HISTORIC PENSACOLA

Colonial Towns and Cities of the Atlantic World

UNIVERSITY PRESS OF FLORIDA

Florida A&M University, Tallahassee

Florida Atlantic University, Boca Raton

Florida Gulf Coast University, Ft. Myers

Florida International University, Miami

Florida State University, Tallahassee

New College of Florida, Sarasota

University of Central Florida, Orlando

University of Florida, Gainesville

University of North Florida, Jacksonville

University of South Florida, Tampa

University of West Florida, Pensacola

COLONIAL TOWNS AND CITIES OF THE ATLANTIC WORLD

Edited by John J. Clune Jr., University of West Florida, and Gregory A. Waselkov, University of South Alabama

Colonial Towns and Cities of the Atlantic World seeks to enhance appreciation for, and understanding of, the rich colonial history and archaeology of towns and cities throughout the Atlantic World.

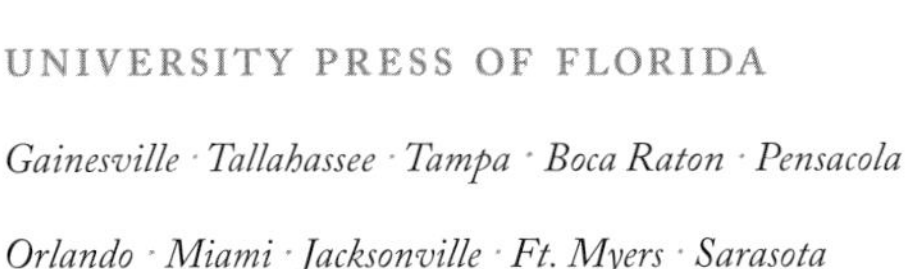

UNIVERSITY PRESS OF FLORIDA

Gainesville · Tallahassee · Tampa · Boca Raton · Pensacola

Orlando · Miami · Jacksonville · Ft. Myers · Sarasota

Historic PENSACOLA

John J. Clune Jr. and Margo S. Stringfield

Printed in the United States of America on acid-free paper

22 21 20 19 18 17 6 5 4 3 2 1

First coth printing, 2009
First paperback printing, 2017

Frontispiece: A View of Pensacola in West Florida by George Gauld, ca. 1765. Library of Congress. Hand colored by Dave Edwards. Courtesy of University of West Florida Archaeology Institute.

Library of Congress Cataloging-in-Publication Data
Clune, John J., Jr. (John James)
Historic Pensacola/John James Clune and Margo S. Stringfield.
p. cm.—(Colonial towns and cities of the Atlantic world)
Includes bibliographical references and index.
ISBN 978-0-8130-3256-6 (cloth: alk. paper)
ISBN 978-0-8130-6450-5 (pbk.)
1. Pensacola (Fla.)—History. I. Stringfield, Margo S. II. Title.
F319.P4C585 2008
975.9'999-dc22 2008015560

The University Press of Florida is the scholarly publishing agency for the State University System of Florida, comprising Florida A&M University, Florida Atlantic University, Florida Gulf Coast University, Florida International University, Florida State University, New College of Florida, University of Central Florida, University of Florida, University of North Florida, University of South Florida, and University of West Florida.

University Press of Florida
15 Northwest 15th Street
Gainesville, FL 32611-2079
http://upress.ufl.edu

CONTENTS

SERIES FOREWORD

Professional historians and archaeologists are engaged in a reconsideration of European colonies in the Americas as components of the overall Atlantic World of the sixteenth to nineteenth centuries. Their studies of individual colonies from a global perspective—as products of the complex interaction of Europeans, Native Americans, and Africans—are revolutionizing academic scholarship. Applying this approach to the local level and packaging new research for a larger audience is the task of this series. At present, consumers of local history must turn to contextualized and enlightening academic scholarship that is often too specialized or to accessible and appealing but parochial popular works that omit broader regional, national, and international perspectives.

This series bridges the worlds of academic scholarship and local history. In this endeavor, our authors paint rich portraits of individual colonial communities, colored by their place in the complex systems of the Atlantic World *and* by the particulars of their natural and social environments. The series' interdisciplinary approach blends the historical and archaeological records of a community's physical, social, economic, and political dimensions in an accessible narrative style. We hope you find the results enjoyable and edifying.

John J. Clune Jr. and Gregory Waselkov

ACKNOWLEDGMENTS

In the sixteenth century, Spanish ships began to bridge the Gulf separating the colony of New Spain (Mexico) and the frontier La Florida. The initial flow of ships, cargo, and people between the ports of Veracruz and Pensacola was just the beginning of a process that connected the Gulf Coast frontier with a worldwide network and initiated one of the most exciting cultural exchanges in what is today the United States of America. Of all U.S. cities, Pensacola has one of the richest cultural heritages. The goal of this book is to share that heritage with the public. Piecing together the tapestry of Pensacola's past is a team effort and would not be possible without the steadfast support and help of many colleagues, family, friends, and students. The authors of this volume are deeply indebted to the faculty and graduate students in archaeology and history at the University of West Florida, whose research efforts add yearly to what we know about our community and its relationship to the wider world.

Individual acknowledgments must begin with pioneers in the fields of Pensacola archaeology and history: Judith Bense and William Coker. With the ardent enthusiasm of an earlier explorer, Judith Bense, the matriarch of Northwest Florida archaeology, has inspired a small army of archaeologists and historians in the study and preservation of the rich cultural resources of Pensacola Bay and its environs. Her vision has brought our community to a better understanding of the value of its heritage. Bense regularly reminds audiences that for many years Pensacola was considered "one of the South's best-kept secrets." The rich pre-Columbian and historical fabrics of the area are secrets no more, owing in large part to the stewardship and vision of Bense and the late historian William Coker, who literally spearheaded the archival search for our Spanish past. His legacy endures in the many books and articles that he published during his lifetime and in the archives he assembled. The combined efforts of Bense and Coker, and those of the many archaeologists and historians who have followed in their footsteps, are bringing long overdue recognition to the first great bay of the Gulf Coast.

Many people had a hand in the production of this volume. The authors wish to thank Greg Waselkov, Bonnie McEwan, and Robin Fabel, who reviewed and commented on the book and whose insights and suggestions were, as always, academically sound and extremely thoughtful. Additionally, we very much appreciate the support of colleagues inside and outside the University of West Florida and students at the university who read one or more of the many drafts of this work. Their efforts made for a more accurate, focused, and structured book. These include John Bratten, Nancy Miller, Dean DeBolt, Norma Harris, Judy Bense, Elizabeth Benchley, John Phillips, John Worth, Jane Dysart, Christina Sherry, Josh Broxson, Betty Vickers, Matt Clavin, Amy Mitchell-Cook, Greg Cook, Gabi Grosse, Bruce Swain, Bob Thomas, and Brenda Rees. Others labored to polish its prose and enhance its reader-friendly tone. Thank you, Anne and Steve.

A great deal of the credit for the look of the book goes to Nancy Miller, who formatted many of the images along with staging set photography, and to Lee McKenzie, who created the digital cartography and graphics. They were indispensable. Faunal analyst and foodways scholar Catherine Parker graciously provided the period recipes and their backgrounds found in each chapter. From the onset, the editors at the University Press of Florida, Eli Bortz, Heather Romans Turci, and Jacqueline Kinghorn Brown, made the entire experience and process a pleasant one and for that we are very indebted.

This book would not have been possible without the support of our families, who were steadfast in their encouragement during a research and writing period that included two hurricanes along with the normal twists and turns of life. Thank you, Allison, Gabrielle, Caroline, John, Gretchen, and Uncle Butz. And thank you, Jim, Beth, and Anne.

Finally, we are deeply indebted to Elizabeth Benchley, Director of the Archaeology Institute, who supported the project and the authors throughout the process. The Archaeology Institute strives to bring the history and archaeology of Pensacola to the public. With the Institute's support, the story continues to be told. Thank you.

HISTORIC PENSACOLA

Introduction

I hereby assert that this bay is the finest jewel possessed by His Majesty . . . not only here in America but in all his kingdom.

—Carlos de Sigüenza y Góngora to the Conde de Galve, Viceroy of Mexico, June 1, 1693

The famous Mexican intellectual, Carlos de Sigüenza, who visited the American Gulf Coast in 1693, recognized in Pensacola Bay the rare qualities that made it a coveted prize in a fierce competition between the great powers of the early modern age—Spain, France, and England—who were waging a struggle for supremacy in the Gulf region and the wider Atlantic World. This book places the bay in these larger contexts, beginning with its initial settlement in 1559 and ending with its forfeiture to the United States in 1821. Rather than offer a complex historical or archaeological analysis of Pensacola Bay and its environs, the book, which draws on both the historical and archaeological record, presents a brief narrative on the same.

Pensacola Bay formed approximately 6,000 years ago following a period of global warming and the melting of polar ice caps. As sea levels rose, the deep valley that evolved into the modern bay filled with water pushing in from the Gulf of Mexico and flowing down the rivers and streams that emptied into the valley. This convergence of waters and sediments resulted in a deep, sheltered bay skirted by sandy marine terraces and backed by extensive wetlands and dense pine forests, interspersed with stands of oak and hickory.[1]

For thousands of years before the arrival of the Europeans, Native Americans moved in and out of the area around Pensacola Bay, hunting deer in the inland forests and harvesting the abundant marine life that thrived in the bay's warm waters. Early Spanish explorers mapped the bay's environs, sounded its depths, charted its anchorages, and recorded their interactions with the native peoples who lived on its shores. Their reports of a sheltered anchorage, natural resources, and resident labor pool convinced officials back in Mexico to settle the area in the mid-sixteenth century. An early, failed attempt to colonize the bay (1559–1561) opened the door to extensive European competition.

Europeans arriving in the seventeenth century found a group of people known as "Panzacola" ("long-haired people") living in the area; these early inhabitants lent their name to both the bay and the modern city of Pensacola. A late-seventeenth- early-eighteenth-century Spanish settlement on Pensacola Bay (1698–1719) did little to discourage French or English designs on the area.

By this date, the French were threatening to colonize the Mississippi Valley from their foothold in the St. Lawrence River Valley and the English had colonized the Atlantic Seaboard. The sparkling bay that captivated Carlos de Sigüenza in 1693 was at the center of a long struggle for empire that changed the course of history in the Gulf region and the broader Atlantic World.

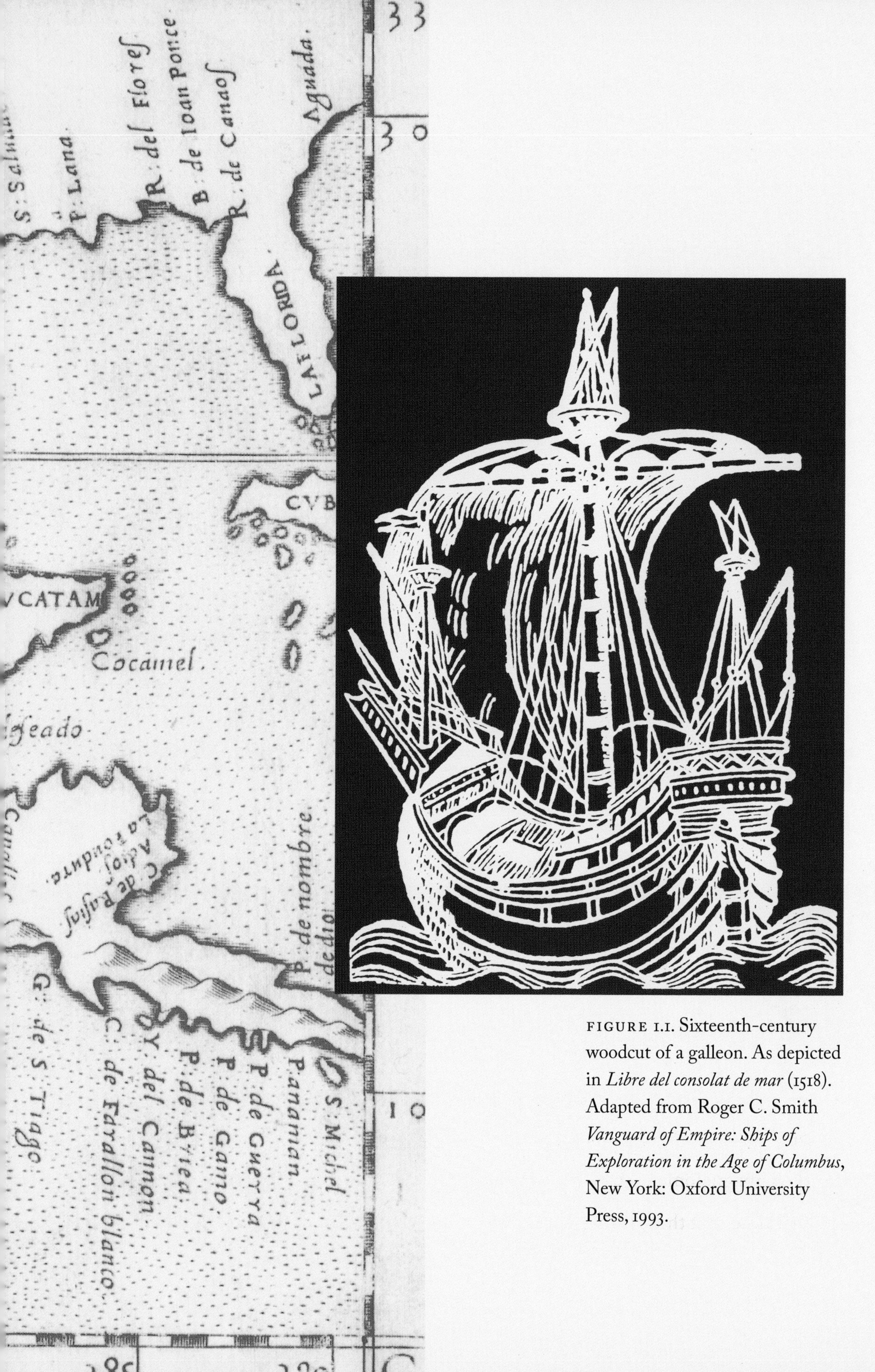

FIGURE 1.1. Sixteenth-century woodcut of a galleon. As depicted in *Libre del consolat de mar* (1518). Adapted from Roger C. Smith *Vanguard of Empire: Ships of Exploration in the Age of Columbus*, New York: Oxford University Press, 1993.

ONE

First Settlement
1559–1561

During the night of the nineteenth of this month of September [1559], there came up from the north a fierce tempest, which, blowing for twenty-four hours from all directions until the same hour as it began, without stopping but increasing continuously, did irreparable damage to the ships of the fleet.

—Tristán de Luna y Arellano, Governor of Florida, to Phillip II, King of Spain, September 24, 1559

In August 1992 nautical archaeologists with the State of Florida were conducting a survey of shipwrecks in Pensacola Bay when their magnetometer signaled an anomaly on the bay floor. It was not the first time that the sensitive device, which detects the distortion of the earth's magnetic field due to the presence of iron objects, had registered something beneath the bay's brackish waters. On this occasion, however, the team of archaeologists led by Roger Smith identified the source of the anomaly to be a ship's anchor. Subsequent investigations proved it to be associated with the wreck of a Spanish galleon, the legendary ship of discovery and conquest. Outfitted with three masts, constructed of heavy oak timbers, and weighing as much as a pair of jet airliners, a galleon could transport more than a hundred people and supplies across an ocean or, in this case, across the Gulf of Mexico.

Archaeologists were initially buoyed by the possibility that they had found a ship from Tristán de Luna y Arellano's 1559 expedition to Pensacola Bay, a settlement attempt that predated the founding of Jamestown by a half century and St. Augustine by a half dozen years. Additional research suggested it was just that, one of the eleven ships that made up an elaborate expedition of colonization conceived and supported by the Viceroy of Mexico and carried out under the auspices of the newly appointed governor of Florida, Tristán de Luna. The ship, however, is no mere relic of a distant Spanish past but an artifact from America's recorded history: that of the European exploration and conquest of the Southeast.

As of 1559, neither the French nor the English had mounted any real threat to Spanish colonies in the New World; they had not achieved the national unity that was necessary to support a program of colonization abroad. French kings to 1559 had little authority over the coastal provinces of France, from

PLATE I.1. Satellite view of Hurricane Ivan approaching the Northern Gulf Coast in September of 2004. National Oceanic and Atmospheric Administration.

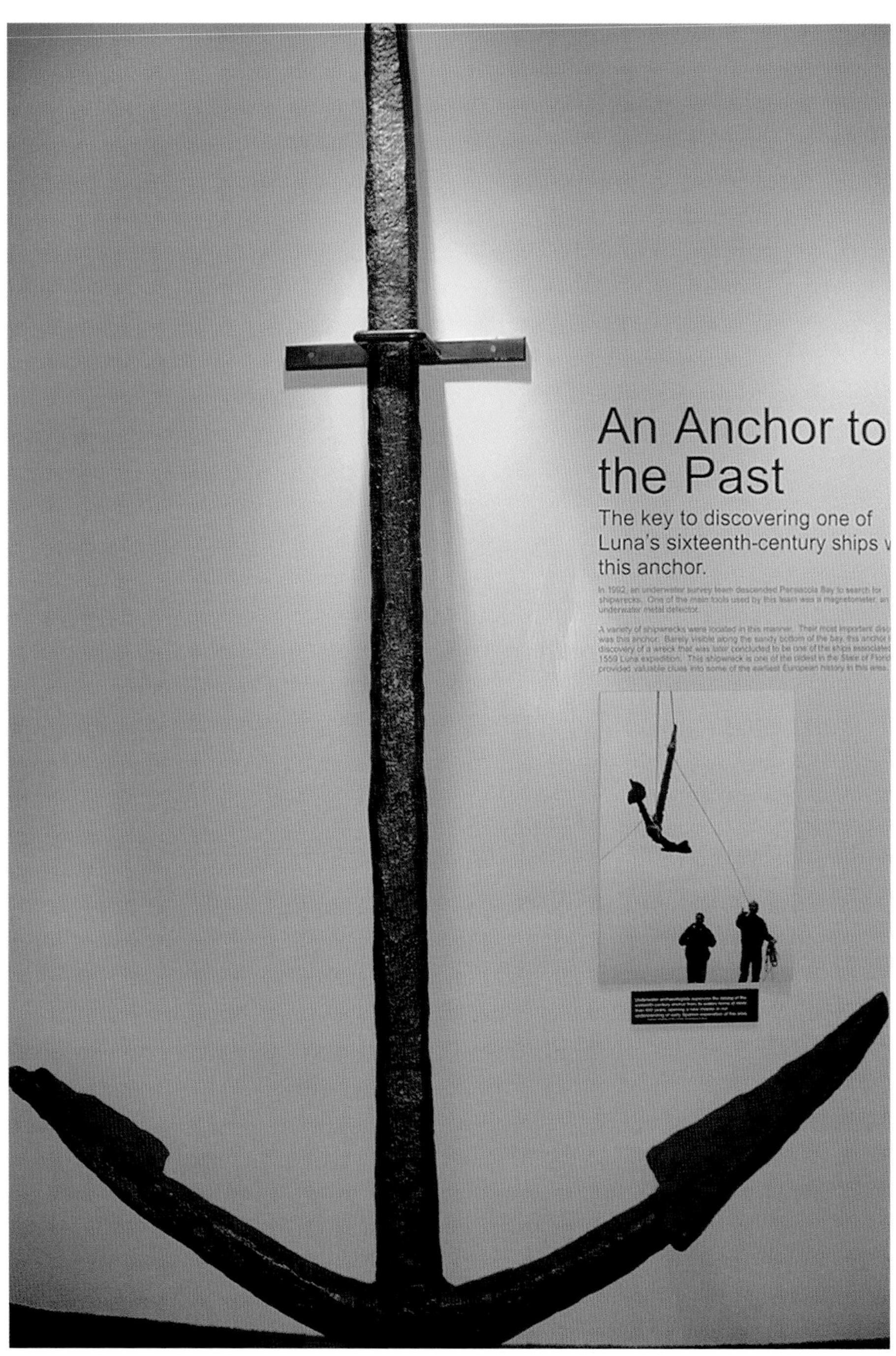

PLATE I.2. The Emanuel Point Ship anchor on display at the T. T. Wentworth Museum, Pensacola. Courtesy of University of West Florida Archaeology Institute.

which a voyage of colonization would have to be staged. And their English counterparts were too preoccupied with questions of faith and dynastic succession, which resulted from a religious reformation in England, to engage in the business of overseas expansion. Spain, by contrast, had achieved a degree of national unity in the fifteenth century with the marriage of the famous Isabella of Castile and Ferdinand of Aragon and the Christian reconquest of the Iberian Peninsula from the Muslims. This unification and consolidation facilitated Spanish colonization efforts overseas.

The empire of the Spanish King Philip II (1556–1598) spanned the Atlantic and included parts of North America, all of Central America and the Caribbean, and much of South America. Early in his reign, however, Philip felt his vast empire threatened by Frenchmen who were trading with Indians along the Carolina coast. This area was strategic because it was located along a route by which Spanish ships carried the wealth of the New World back to Spain. The coastline was also part of Philip's birthright, the fringes of La Florida: a vast, ill-defined, and unsettled expanse first claimed by Ponce de León in 1513. In Ponce's wake, Spaniards tried to make good on his claim. Among those was Pánfilo de Narváez, who may have been among the first Europeans to visit Pensacola Bay.

NVEVA HISPANI
G
250
255
260
265
33
30
25
20
15
10
R: Tontonteanc
P: Tabursa
Puertos
B. Secondido
Cinola
S: Franc
R: Albofeda
MAR VERMEIO
B: de S. +
Basos
B: Canoas
Ancoras
B: de S. Abad
Vandras
Ciguata
S: Tiago
Agnataneo
Balenas
C. +
S. Tomas
MAR DEL SVR

FIGURE 1.2. Map, *Nueva Hispania Tabula Nova*. Ruscelli. 1561. Showing location of Veracruz (area of *Villa Rica*), Mexico, and general area of Pensacola, Florida (approximately between *S. Salvador* and *P. Lana*). Courtesy of University of Florida, George A. Smathers Library, Special Collections.

Road to Pensacola Bay, 1528–1559

In 1528, Pánfilo de Narváez came ashore near St. Petersburg, Florida, with some 300 men and proceeded overland to an area around Tallahassee, known as the Land of the Apalachee. There, the fertile soils of the Tallahassee Hills supported a large and powerful Indian culture. Narváez and his men hoped to find gold and silver there. What they found were natives who were neither pleased by their arrival nor willing to part with precious food stores. Weary of the relentless Indian attacks and short on supplies, Narváez made his way to the coast. In the absence of waiting ships, he ordered his men to build rafts. Thereafter, the expedition set off in a westerly direction in hopes of reaching Mexico. Whether the makeshift flotilla visited Pensacola Bay is open to speculation. A sheltered harbor to the west of Apalachee provided refuge to Narvaéz and his men during a storm, and Indians living nearby provided them with dried fish and water. The hospitality of the native hosts was short-lived, however, as they soon fell upon the European visitors, wounding many of them, including Narváez, and forcing a hasty departure.

A storm subsequently scattered Narváez's hobbled vessels off the Texas coast. In the end, only four survivors made their way back to Mexico including Estevanico ("Stephen the Moor"), generally considered the first African explorer of North America, and the famous Álvaro Núñez Cabeza de Vaca. When Cabeza de Vaca spurned an invitation of Hernando de Soto to return to Florida, the latter took it upon himself to tame the wilds of the American

Southeast and to tap its fabled wealth. The Soto expedition (1539–1543) provided the first firm evidence of Europeans on Pensacola Bay.

Hernando de Soto led a large expedition to Florida in 1539. Comprising some 600 soldiers, the expedition came ashore near Tampa Bay. Like Narváez, Soto ventured to the area around Tallahassee. Encamped there for the winter, he sent one of his lieutenants, Francisco Maldonado, west to find a good harbor that could be used as a re-supply point. Maldonado selected Pensacola Bay and returned to the bay often in hopes of reuniting with his leader, but there would be no reunion. Before Soto died of a fever in 1542 he had wandered far to the west of Pensacola, crossing the Mississippi River and venturing as far north as Arkansas. In 1543, the remnants of his expedition struggled back to Mexico with little to show for their efforts. Spanish claims to Florida were as tenuous as when Soto had set out four years earlier. The expedition did, however, feed the myth of a rich Indian kingdom in the interior Southeast known as Coosa.

Several elements came together to send the Spanish back to Florida in 1559. Coosa and the agricultural potential of the interior were factors, as were persistent rumors of silver and gold, a concern for shipwreck victims who faced almost certain death along Florida's coasts, a desire to spread the Catholic faith and baptize natives, and the belief that the French had their sights set on Santa Elena, a mysterious but nonetheless strategic location on Port Royal Sound, South Carolina.[1] Spanish officials were concerned that the French might use Santa Elena as a base from which to raid the outbound Spanish

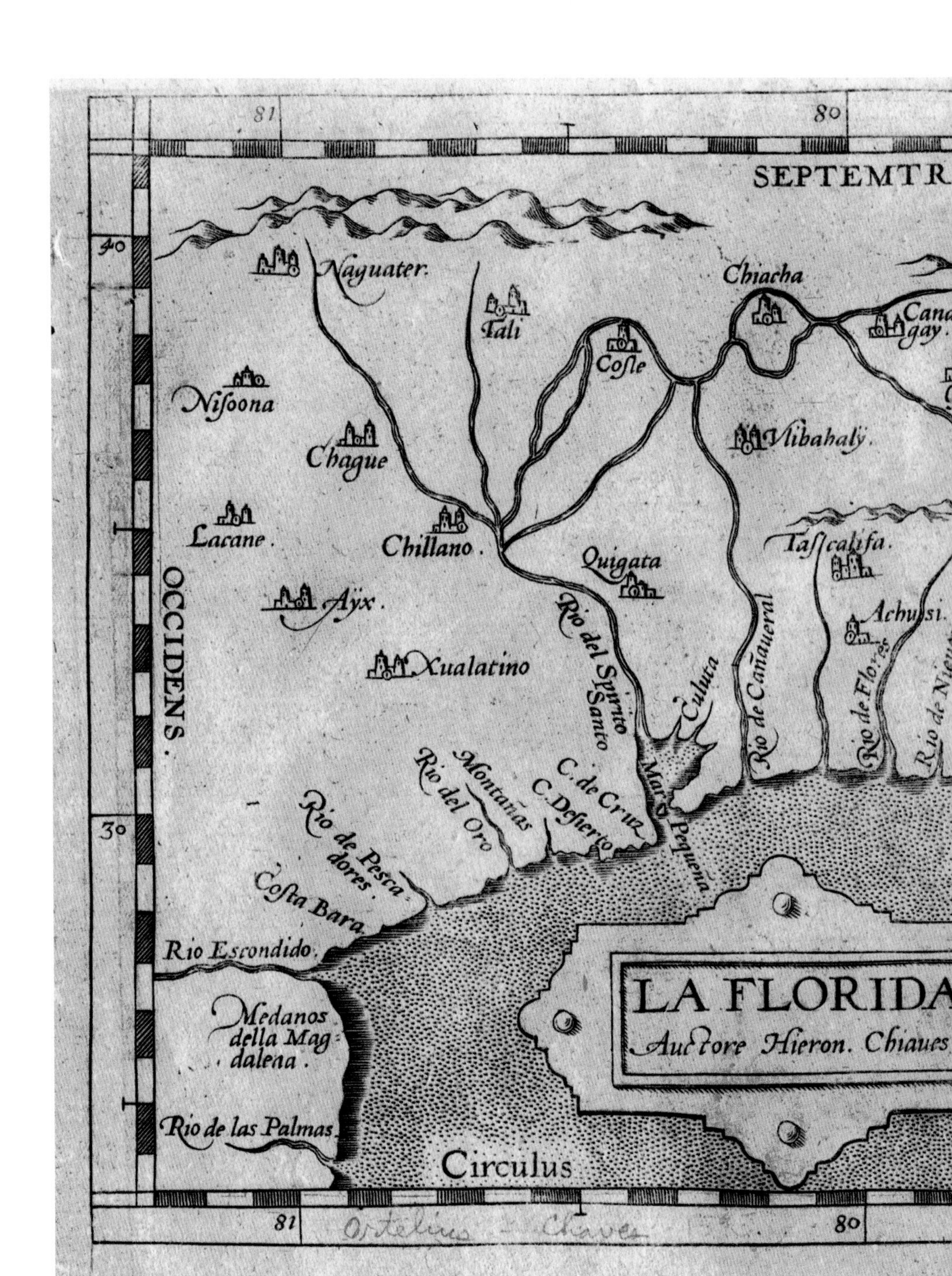
81
80
SEPTEMTR
40
Naguater.
Tali
Chiacha
Cana
gay.
Coste
Nisoona
Chague
Vlibahaly.
Lacane.
Chillano.
Tasscalifa.
Quigata
OCCIDENS.
Ayx.
Achu
Xualatino
Rio del Spirito Santo
Culuta
Rio de Cañaueral
Rio de Flores
Montañas
Rio del Oro
C. de Cruz
C. Desierto
Mar Pequeña
30
Rio de Pesca dores.
Costa Bara.
Rio Escondido.
Medanos della Magdalena.
Rio de las Palmas.
Circulus
LA FLORIDA
Auctore Hieron. Chiaues
81
80
Ortelius - Chaves

FIGURE 1.3. La Florida. From Abraham Ortelius, *Additamentum to the Theatrum Orbis Terrarum*, 1584. Showing general location of Pensacola Bay (*P. de Santa Maria*) and Santa Elena (*P[unta] S[anta] Helena*) on the eastern seaboard. Courtesy of University of Florida, George Smathers Library, Special Collections. Hand colored by Nancy Miller.

treasure fleet that passed just offshore or to access the wealth of northern Mexico. A network of roads that linked, at least mythically, Santa Elena and the silver-mining town of Zacatecas made the latter possible. The fact that Soto made use of a native system of trails during his three-year expedition convinced Spanish officials that such a road, or roads, existed.

Peninsular Florida and the Southeast were "connected" in a sense by an extensive trail system, one that was part of a pan-regional trade network linking prehistoric cultures across a broad region. (See Figures 1.2 and 1.3) Archaeologists have found evidence of an active interchange of ideas and materials across Florida, up into Georgia, through the Carolinas, and to destinations farther west. While the archaeological record suggests far-reaching contact among pre-Columbian peoples, it does not delineate a major artery linking Santa Elena with the distant Zacatecas, over a thousand miles away.

The plan formulated by Mexican Viceroy Luis de Velasco in 1557–1558 was to utilize this system of trails to colonize the Carolina coast from the Gulf of Mexico. The idea was to found a town on the north central Gulf Coast, a second at Coosa in northwest Georgia or northeast Alabama, and a third at Santa Elena. That the viceroy, a learned man, proposed such a settlement scheme can be understood only in the context of the time, one in which navigation was still more art than science and longitude was little more than an educated guess. Sailing around the tip of Florida and through the Florida Straits was always time-consuming and occasionally treacherous. Moreover, finding Santa Elena from the sea could be difficult as few knew where it was or what it looked like. Finally, the coveted locale was thought to be only about 250 miles from the north central Gulf Coast. The straight-line distance from Pensacola to Port Royal Sound is about 350 miles, but a direct route is impractical due to many natural barriers.

The viceroy needed, at the very least, a gifted colonizer to put this elaborate plan into action, but his choice of Tristán de Luna proved as flawed as the plan itself. The image of Luna that emerges from the pages of Herbert Ingram Priestly's classic *Tristán De Luna: Conquistador of the Old South* is that of a man with the pedigree, wealth, and experience but neither the demeanor nor the judgment to be a successful colonizer. He was from an old and monied Castilian family and had married into wealth. The third husband of a wealthy widow, Luna had the resources necessary to undertake the venture. Related to the conquistador Hernán Cortés through marriage and to the first Mexican Viceroy, Antonio de Mendoza, by blood, he had the connections to do so. And having served in Mexico for three decades prior to 1559, he had the experience. Luna was best known for serving as second in command to Franciscan Vásquez de Coronado on the latter's two-year expedition to the American Southwest (1540–1542).[2] That service marked the highlight of his career.

In preparation for sending Luna to the northern Gulf coast, Viceroy Velasco sent out two reconnaissance expeditions in 1558. The first expedition, commanded by Guido de Lavezaris, departed from Veracruz in September and explored the Gulf Coast eastward of the Mississippi River,

Mobile Bay, however, with its abundant pine and oak; nuts and fruits; fish; shellfish; fields of corn, beans, and squash; and open lands for grazing cattle and horses appealed most to the Spanish ship captain. Upon his return to Veracruz in mid-December, Lavezaris presumably proclaimed Mobile Bay the best place for a base settlement. Late that same month, an expedition captained by Juan de Rentería departed Veracruz for the Gulf Coast. Stopping briefly in Havana, Rentería explored the coast in a counterclockwise fashion, from Apalachee Bay westward to Pensacola and Mobile. He returned to Veracruz in early 1559 a strong proponent of Pensacola Bay.[3] Events were already in motion to send a large expedition to the Gulf Coast, be it to Mobile or Pensacola.

On November 1, 1558, Tristán de Luna arrived at the large cathedral on the Plaza Mayor in Mexico City to take his oath of office as "Governor and Captain General of La Florida and Santa Elena." In the months following the ceremony, the anointed leader of Florida turned his attention to enlisting soldiers, settlers, artisans, priests, and Aztec warriors for his Florida venture, but on this day, the feast of All Saints, all attention focused on Luna.[4] To the military, religious, and civil dignitaries of the city gathered on that day, the future security of the empire seemed to rest on the shoulders of this experienced, well-connected, and wealthy Spaniard and on his ability to carve a colony out of the Florida wilderness.

On June 11, 1559, Luna sailed from Veracruz at the head of one of the most formidable settlement expeditions in American history: a twelve-ship fleet carrying in excess of 1,500 persons, more than double the number on any previous Spanish expedition to Florida and many times the combined number that the English sent to Roanoke, Jamestown, and Plymouth. Viceroy Velasco, in fact, thought the expedition too large to be effective, judging there to be too many wives and children of soldiers and far too many camp followers.

The voyage to Pensacola Bay started well enough with two and a half weeks of good winds, following the route of Lavezaris to the shoals north of Yucatán. After more mishaps, the fleet reached Mobile Bay in late July. There, Luna offloaded some of his men and 130 surviving horses (240 began the voyage) to be driven overland. Reaching Pensacola Bay (Ochuse) on August 14 or 15, 1559, which coincided with the feast of the Assumption of Mary, Luna christened the bay Bahía Santa María Filipina after the Virgin Mary and King Philip II of Spain. He subsequently chose a high site overlooking the bay for the location of the settlement.[5]

With a finite food supply on hand and no immediate prospects of growing food, Luna's men quickly set out to find the native populations that a generation of earlier explorers had placed in the area. But they were nowhere to be found. European diseases introduced by previous Spanish expeditions, particularly that of Soto, may have decimated native populations around the bay. Whatever the culprit, the absence of a native population base to depend on for provisions and labor complicated matters. After all, the colonists hardly had time to plant, and even if they had, the sandy soil in and around

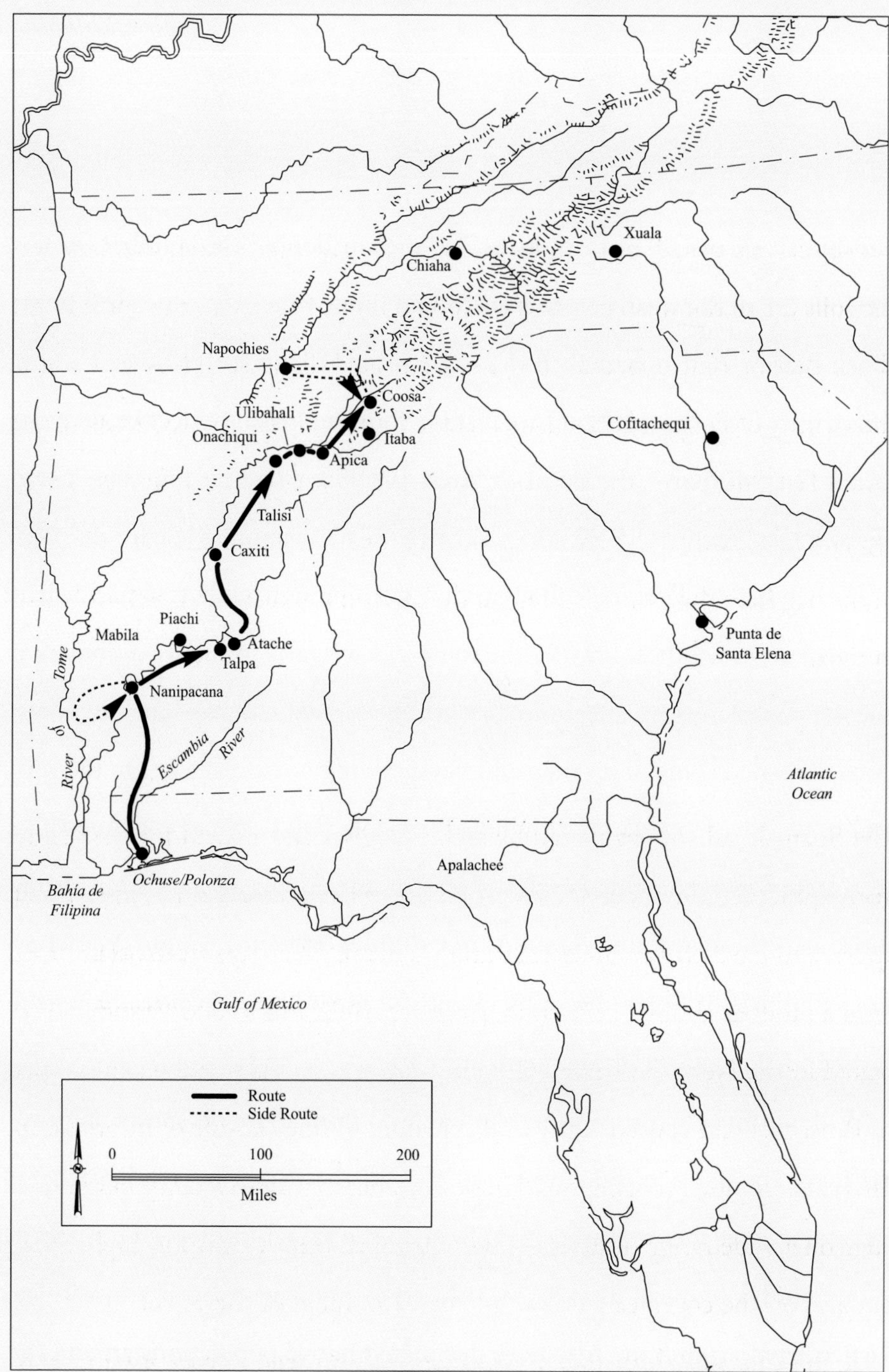

FIGURE 1.4. Approximate route inland from Pensacola showing the general area of Coosa, Nanipacana, and Santa Elena. Adapted from *First Encounters: Spanish Explorations in the Caribbean and United States, 1492–1570*, edited by Jerald T. Milanich and Susan Milbrath. Gainesville: University Press of Florida, 1989.

Pensacola was simply not conducive to large-scale agriculture. The most fertile soils are to the west, nearer the Mobile-Tensaw Delta, to the north in the Black Belt of Alabama, and to the east in the Tallahassee Hills area, not in the vicinity of Pensacola Bay. Luna had to find an alternative food source and find it fast. Moreover, the situation worsened dramatically on September 19, 1559, when a hurricane destroyed almost all the food supplies aboard the ships in the bay, including those stored on the galleon discovered by archaeologists in 1992.

Broken Lifeline

The Spanish galleon excavated by archaeologists and named for the nearby geographical landmark on the eastern shore of Escambia Bay, Emanuel Point, appears to have broken anchor during the September 1559 storm and surged onto a sandbar about a mile from the point. Built in the Old World and repaired in the New, the Emanuel Point Ship was an old vessel when it sailed to Pensacola and subsequently sank, creating a time capsule of information. This catastrophic event captured in one moment in time expands our knowledge on a wide range of topics—not only on sixteenth-century shipbuilding but also on the complex cultural microenvironment of the vessel.

Archaeologists glean much information from wood types used in construction episodes. Advances in science and technology over the last twenty years have facilitated their efforts to determine places of origin and repair. The application of physical and chemical sciences to artifact analysis and conservation are among the most important of these breakthroughs. These include x-ray imaging of artifacts, metallurgical and ballast analyses, and botanical and faunal species verification. Although time-consuming and expensive, scientific analysis of the Emanuel Point demonstrated that the ship embodies both Old and New World components.

The architectural plans of sixteenth- and seventeenth-century ships are rare, but archaeologists were able to compare the Emanuel Point Ship to other sixteenth-century shipwrecks and to ships depicted in artwork of the time. (See Figure 1.1.) There was no question: this was an authentic Spanish galleon. If there had been any doubt, archaeologists found a small carved rendering of a Spanish galleon amid the wreckage of the Emanuel Point. Looking like a child's plaything, the wooden silhouette was discovered in the ship's bilge pump. A sixteenth-century Spanish shipwright may have carved the tiny galleon during a break from his labors, only to lose it and have it appear in an American archaeological assemblage 450 years later.[6]

Other artifacts recovered from the wreck of the Emanuel Point Ship represent a broad spectrum of materials transported on a sixteenth-century ship of colonization. Along with humans, their cargo, and their farm animals traveled a number of small stowaways: cockroaches, mice, and black rats, Old World insects and rodents introduced into the New World in the wake of the Spanish conquest. The recovery of the remains of cockroaches and black rats marks one of the earliest archaeologically documented cases of their presence in North America.

PLATE 1.3. Extant hull remains of the Emanuel Point Ship exposed during excavations. Courtesy of Florida Bureau of Archaeological Research.

PLATE 1.4. Reproduction of the carved wood silhouette of a sixteenth-century galleon recovered from the bilge pump of the ship, example of the ship's hardware, and ballast stones. Courtesy of University of West Florida Archaeology Institute.

Archaeologists have linked other artifacts to the humans who traveled aboard the ship. Fragments of colorful Aztec "face" jars from Central Mexico and obsidian blades, which the Aztecs embedded in wooden clubs to make them more deadly, are evidence of the 100 Aztec warriors that accompanied Luna to Pensacola. A small leather sole from a platform shoe probably belonged to one of the women onboard; although children are known to have been on the voyage, archaeologists have yet to find physical evidence of their presence. However, artifacts recovered from the galley of the ship are items

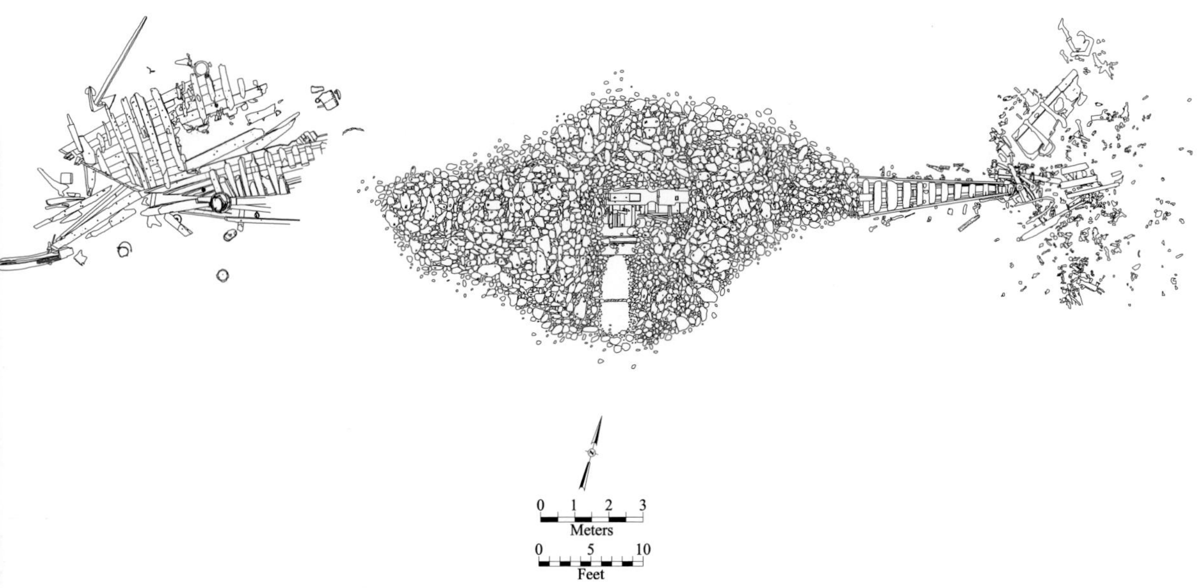

FIGURE 1.5. Site plan of the Emanuel Point Ship. Courtesy of University of West Florida Archaeology Institute.

PLATE 1.5. Recovering a sherd of Aztec pottery from the Emanuel Point Ship. Courtesy of Florida Bureau of Archaeological Research.

PLATE 1.6. Aztec wave pottery (*negro grafito sombre rojo pulido*) sherd following conservation treatment. Sherd is from a pottery vessel, shaped like a human head, that was made in the Central Valley of Mexico. Courtesy of University of West Florida Archaeology Institute.

that could have been used in the preparation of meals. These include Mexican tableware, storage jars, copper cooking pots and pans, a mortar and pestle, and even food remains—items that a soldier's wife might also have utilized in setting up a household kitchen in Pensacola.

The botanical assemblage also includes a variety of fruit, seeds, and nuts that illustrate the fusion of New and Old World cultures in the kitchen. Persimmon and papaya are New World foods likely grown in and around

PLATE 1.7. Bronze pestle being excavated from the shipwreck. Courtesy of Bureau of Archaeological Research.

Veracruz. Almonds, olives, hazelnuts, cherries, and plums are Old World cultigens and Iberian favorites more than likely shipped from Spain to Veracruz then loaded on the ships bound for Pensacola. The bones of Old World domesticates, such as pigs, goats, cows, sheep, and chickens, are also in evidence. Historical documents provide additional detail about items that do not appear in the archaeological record due to decomposition. These include corn, wheat flour, hardtack, salt pork, bacon, dried beef, cheese, oil, wine, and vinegar that would have served as staples of a colonist's diet.

Based on available documents, it is uncertain how much the colonists supplemented their meager diets with the most readily available food source: the fish and shellfish so abundant in the bay, rivers, and streams of the area. The colonists did return to the coast specifically so that they could fish, and long nets were purchased for the expedition. The colonists, however, may have had a disdain for the taste of local seafood, such as mullet and oysters; in Spain, certain freshwater fish and deepwater fish like cod, tuna, and anchovies were the seafood of choice.[7] Faunal specialist Catherine Parker notes that wild foods often were not staples of the Spanish diet, and that typically only the poor in society consumed small mammals and birds, fish, and shellfish. Another factor may have been that those who accompanied Luna were simply inept fishermen. They were, after all, recruited from interior towns and villages in Mexico, not from the coast. They lived off the land, not the sea. Although these first settlers looked to the land for their sustenance, they looked to the town for their culture.

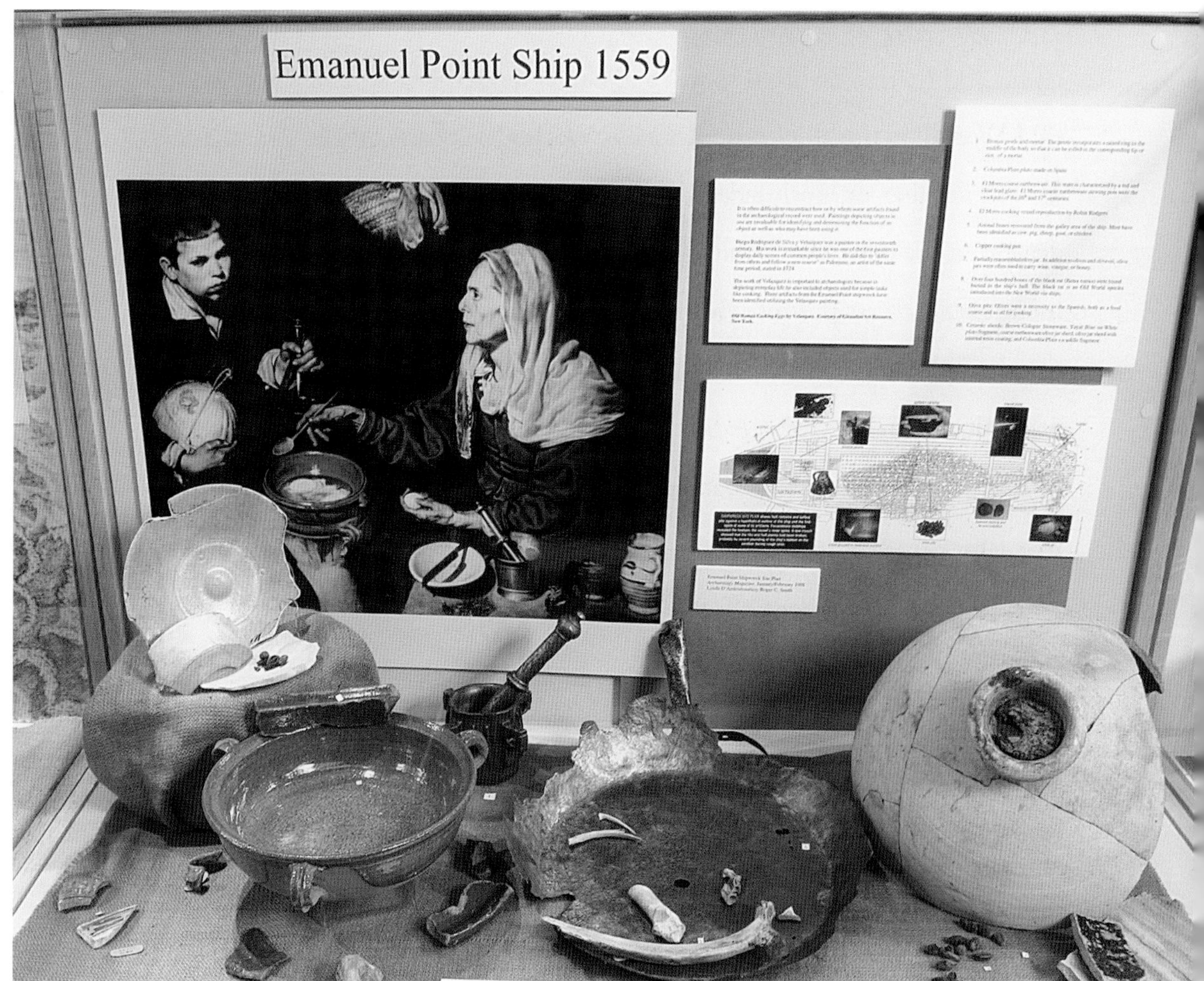

PLATE 1.8. Exhibit of artifacts recovered from the galley area of the ship and a reproduction of a cooking pot (*El Moro* ware) based on recovered sherds. The backdrop of *Old Woman Cooking Eggs* (1618) by Diego Rodríguez de Silva y Velázquez illustrates how the artifacts would have been used in the sixteenth and early seventeenth centuries. Original painting in the National Gallery, Edinburgh. Courtesy of University of West Florida Archaeology Institute.

Settlement

Old World, Spanish culture, like New World, Mexican culture, was urban. Town planning on both sides of the Atlantic was hardly a haphazard endeavor. In the New World, a comprehensive set of ordinances guided settlement efforts. First promulgated in 1513, the ordinances governed all aspects of urban planning and grew in time to include some 3,000 laws. From the beginning, the laws dictated that colonizers conform to the established concept of a Spanish town. Based on early Roman models, a Spanish town was laid out on a grid pattern, with religious and government buildings on a central plaza, and prominent residents living as close to the center as possible.

Historian Charles Arnade notes that the main aspects of town planning at Pensacola were security, sustainability, and proximity to the water. In accordance with Spanish ordinances and the viceroy's specific instructions, Luna planned a town of 140 lots. Religious and government buildings—the church, governor's house, royal treasury, and others—were planned for forty choice lots at the center of the settlement. Other lots were reserved for inns, warehouses, jails, and slaughterhouses. Most, however, were intended for 100 heads of households who were to defend the town and were to venture out each day to farm adjacent lands. However, the great majority of the soldiers and settlers were destined for the planned towns at Coosa and Santa Elena, not for Pensacola.[8]

Given the catastrophic hurricane that impacted the settlement attempt, Luna realized little, if any, of the formal town that Spanish ordinances and the viceroy's orders called for. Moreover, Luna's vague description of the settlement's location in a letter to Philip II—"a high point of land which slopes down to the bay where the ships come to anchor for settlement"—provides few clues of the town's location and much less about its layout. Researchers have found the site of Luna's settlement in the heart of Pensacola. There, they are learning more about the first settlers.

Settlers

One source that researchers look to for information on settlers is the *Codex Osuna*, a collection of Aztec pictographs and ideograms with Spanish translations, which date to 1565. A portion of the codex details a suit brought by the families of the 100 Aztec warriors who ventured to Pensacola with Luna. The claimants contended that their fathers and brothers were never paid for the services that they rendered to the Crown.[9] Aside from the sparse information that can be gleaned from this early indigenous document, we know little about the Aztecs who accompanied Luna. We know even less about the other settlers.

In a letter to Luna, Viceroy Velasco condemned the colonists as a "large group of half-breeds, mulattoes, and Indians [who] will only serve to set the camp in confusion and eat up the supplies." In condemning the lower-class elements of the expedition, the Spanish official reflected the bias of his day as much as the demeanor of the colonists. He would have preferred *peninsulares*, Spaniards born in Spain, to populate his new colony. He would have settled for *criollos*, Spaniards born in the New World. What he got were a good number of mestizos (Spanish-Indian race mixture), mulattos (Spanish-African), Indians, and Africans. This is hardly surprising, as these individuals would have been among those most anxious to escape the poverty and degradation of a Mexican society dominated by Spanish landowners, bureaucrats, and priests. Finally, there were the officers and bureaucrats who represented the elite of frontier society. Unfortunately for the elite, Mother Nature's fury knows no social class.

Survival

In the aftermath of the devastating hurricane of September 19, 1559, Luna dispatched a surviving ship to Veracruz to alert authorities of the disaster and to secure emergency supplies. Unfortunately, there were few supplies to be found in the Mexican port city during the summer rainy season when daily downpours made roads impassable and isolated the coast from its fertile and productive hinterland. In the interim, Luna sent search parties out from Pensacola into the interior to scour the countryside for food. One party stumbled upon an Indian town above the headwaters of the Escambia River on the banks of the Alabama River named Nanipacana.

Luna had to act decisively if he had any hope of saving the colony. In February 1560, Luna left a skeleton crew of about 100 people at Pensacola and moved the main party north to the Indian town. Half-starved soldiers and settlers reached Nanipacana expecting to find relief, only to discover that the hundred or so native residents had packed up their food stores and fled. The colonists were back to an all-too-familiar diet of acorns, herbs, and roots. In April 1560, the desperate leader sent his second in command, Mateo del Sauz, in search of the fabled Coosa. Among the 200 or so who accompanied Sauz were men who had traveled with Soto two decades before. Also in the Sauz party were Luna's nephew, Captain Cristóbal Ramírez de Arellano, and the Dominican priests, Domingo de Anunciación and Domingo de Salazar. The men departed with few food supplies and found little en route. In desperation, they began to eat their horses and whatever cowhide was available, even their own boots. What they did not consume, they bartered with Indians for food. Only stands of chestnut and walnut trees slowed the rate at which the men consumed or bartered away their attire. In July 1560, Sauz finally reached Coosa. Disappointed by what he found there—the largest town had only a few hundred residents—Sauz sent Luna's nephew, Captain Ramírez de Arellano, to retrieve his uncle so that he could see Coosa for himself.[10] (See figure 1.4.)

Luna, having abandoned Nanipacana to return to Pensacola the previous month to await supplies, and suffering from bouts of fever and delirium that are suggestive of malaria, could not rally the men in camp for another adventure into the interior. As the months passed, relief ships were few and the governor's mental faculties further deteriorated. In the midst of Luna's worsening condition, the king ordered him to immediately settle Santa Elena. With so much at stake, the increasingly insecure governor pinned all of his hopes on another nephew, Martín Doz. In August 1560, Luna outfitted the inexperienced Doz with three or four vessels and between fifty and sixty men and sent him in search of Santa Elena. Near Havana, a storm scattered Doz's ships, dooming both nephew and uncle to failure.[11]

Luna's Last Days

On the heels of the Doz debacle, the Sauz party returned from Coosa, and Pedro de Feria, a Dominican priest who was among the hundreds of colonists who escaped Pensacola aboard relief ships returning to Veracruz, briefed the viceroy on the mutinous situation on the coast. By January 1561, Velasco had heard enough. Concluding that Luna was unlikely to advance beyond his tenuous foothold on Pensacola Bay, the viceroy named Angel de Villafañe the new governor of Florida and Santa Elena and sent him to relieve the troubled leader. In the interim between Villafañe's appointment and his arrival in Pensacola, Pedro de Feria's Dominican brethren on the bay, Domingo de Anunciación and Domingo de Salazar, fueled the mutiny by effectively excommunicating

Luna. They barred the governor from the church lest he reconcile with dissident officers who were calling for an end to the Florida venture. Mercifully, Villafañe reached Pensacola in April 1561, and Luna quickly departed for Havana and subsequently for Spain.[12]

The new governor arrived with a new plan. Leaving about sixty soldiers at Pensacola, he ferried the balance of the settlement's population to Havana (the population of Pensacola in the spring of 1561 had dwindled to between 160 and 200 desperate souls) and recruited an expedition of about 100 to go in search of Santa Elena. Tormented by storms, one of which sank two of his four ships, and with no real interest in an Atlantic colony, Villafañe abandoned Santa Elena not long after he arrived in July 1561 and by August had withdrawn the last troops from Pensacola. Finally, in February 1562, the Viceroy of New Spain made the decision to put an end to a settlement attempt gone awry.

Less than a year later, in April 1562, Jean Ribaut confirmed Spanish fears by founding the French Huguenot settlement of Charlesfort on Port Royal Sound, at Santa Elena. Within a year, Ribaut's fledgling settlement had failed, but he inspired another. Frenchmen René Goulaine de Laudonnière established Fort Caroline at the mouth of the St. John's River in 1564. The Spaniard Pedro Menéndez de Avilés subsequently destroyed Fort Caroline and founded St. Augustine in 1565. With the founding of "America's First City," Luna's 1559 settlement on Pensacola Bay faded into memory. For the next 133 years (1565–1698), Spanish officials neglected to settle what many still considered to be the best natural harbor in the New World.

Summary

Tristán de Luna and Pensacola are not household names in American history. However, for over seventy years, historians have mined Spanish and Mexican archives in hopes of learning more about the initial colonization attempt. Currently, UWF archaeologists are investigating three shipwrecks from the Luna fleet. Historians are doing their own excavations in the Spanish and Mexican archives—uncovering new documents related to the Luna Expedition and re-examining known documents. These researchers are hopeful that future discovering in distant archives, beneath the ground of Pensacola, and under the waters of its bay will round out our understanding of this ephemeral attempt at settlement and survival on the Gulf Coast frontier of La Florida.

After departing Pensacola, Tristán de Luna spent six years in Spain and the final six in Mexico, trying to redeem his reputation and restore his fortune. He accomplished neither and languished in his last years as a forgotten and impoverished man. Luna died in Mexico City on September 16, 1573, three days short of the fourteenth anniversary of the devastating hurricane that destroyed his fledgling settlement on Pensacola Bay. His legacy lives on in the history, archaeology, and culture of Pensacola.

The authors extend their deep appreciation to Dr. John Worth who has graciously assisted in updating this chapter based on current research.

RECIPE: Hardtack

One of the mainstays of Luna's rations, hardtack, survives in the modern culinary tradition of Pensacola as the main ingredient in a local specialty, "gaspache," a salad made with the New-World cultigens tomatoes and bell peppers (see chapter 5 for the gaspache recipe). Hardtack is thick, cracker-like bread made of flour, salt, and water. After kneading and shaping, it is baked until almost all of the moisture in the mixture is eliminated. When properly made and stored, it will last for several years. Because it could be made so cheaply and lasted so long, hardtack was a nutritious, convenient food for soldiers, sailors, explorers, or anyone else in the colonial era who had to move quickly over long distances through unfamiliar surroundings. When freshly baked bread was not available, hardtack was an integral part of most standard military rations.

Hardtack had two major drawbacks. When the biscuit was fresh and hard, it was literally too hard for persons with bad gums and teeth (or no teeth) to bite and chew. It had to be crumbled into stew, broth, water, or some other liquid to soften before being eaten. But if the hardtack became wet or damp during storage, the biscuits would mold—and possibly become infested with weevils and maggots. Many wry jokes were made about these little insects being part of the "fresh meat" ration!

4 cups plain white or whole-wheat flour (or a mixture of each type)

4 teaspoons salt

Clean water (have 2 cups measured)

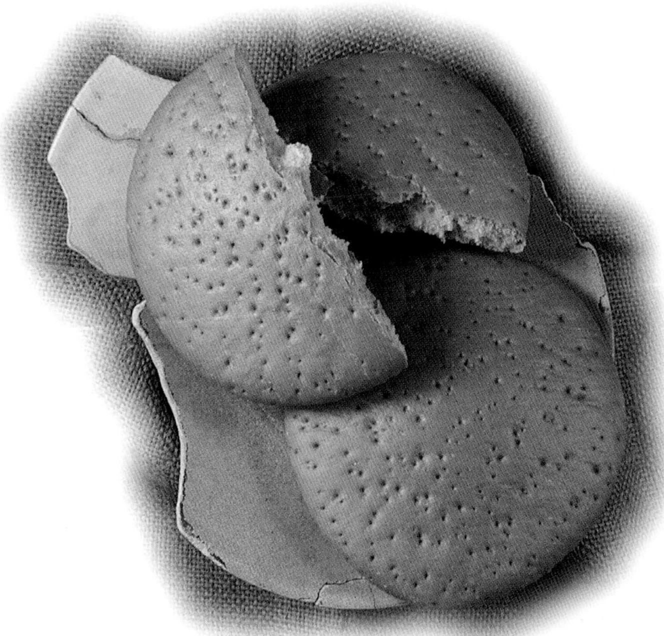

Mix flour with salt in a large bowl. Gradually add just enough water to bind ingredients together, forming a stiff dough (dough should not stick to the hands, rolling pin, or baking pan). Knead well. On a lightly floured surface, roll out the dough into a rectangle about ½ inch thick. Cut into 3-inch × 3-inch squares; prick a pattern of four rows of four holes into each square using a new nail or other pointed object. Turn each square over and prick that side, as well. Do not pierce holes all the way through the dough.

Place the squares of hardtack on an ungreased cookie sheet and bake in a 375° F oven for thirty minutes. Turn each square over and bake for an additional twenty to thirty minutes; the squares should be slightly brown on both sides. Turn oven off; with door left ajar, let hardtack cool on the pan. The squares should be hard and dry as bricks. Yield: Ten squares—background and recipe by Catherine Parker.

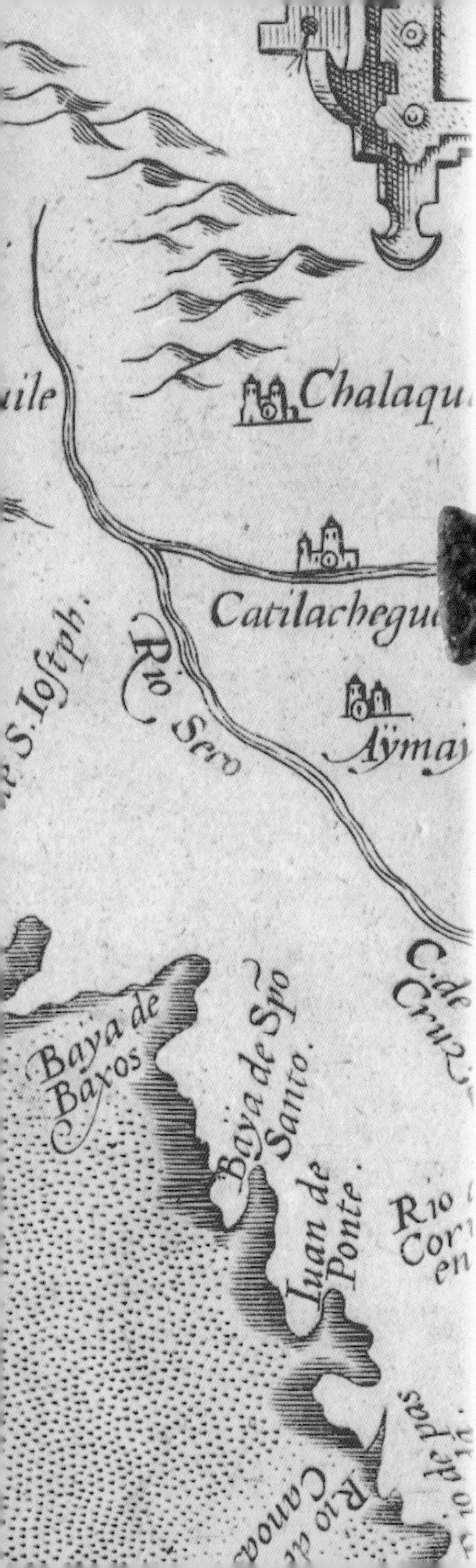

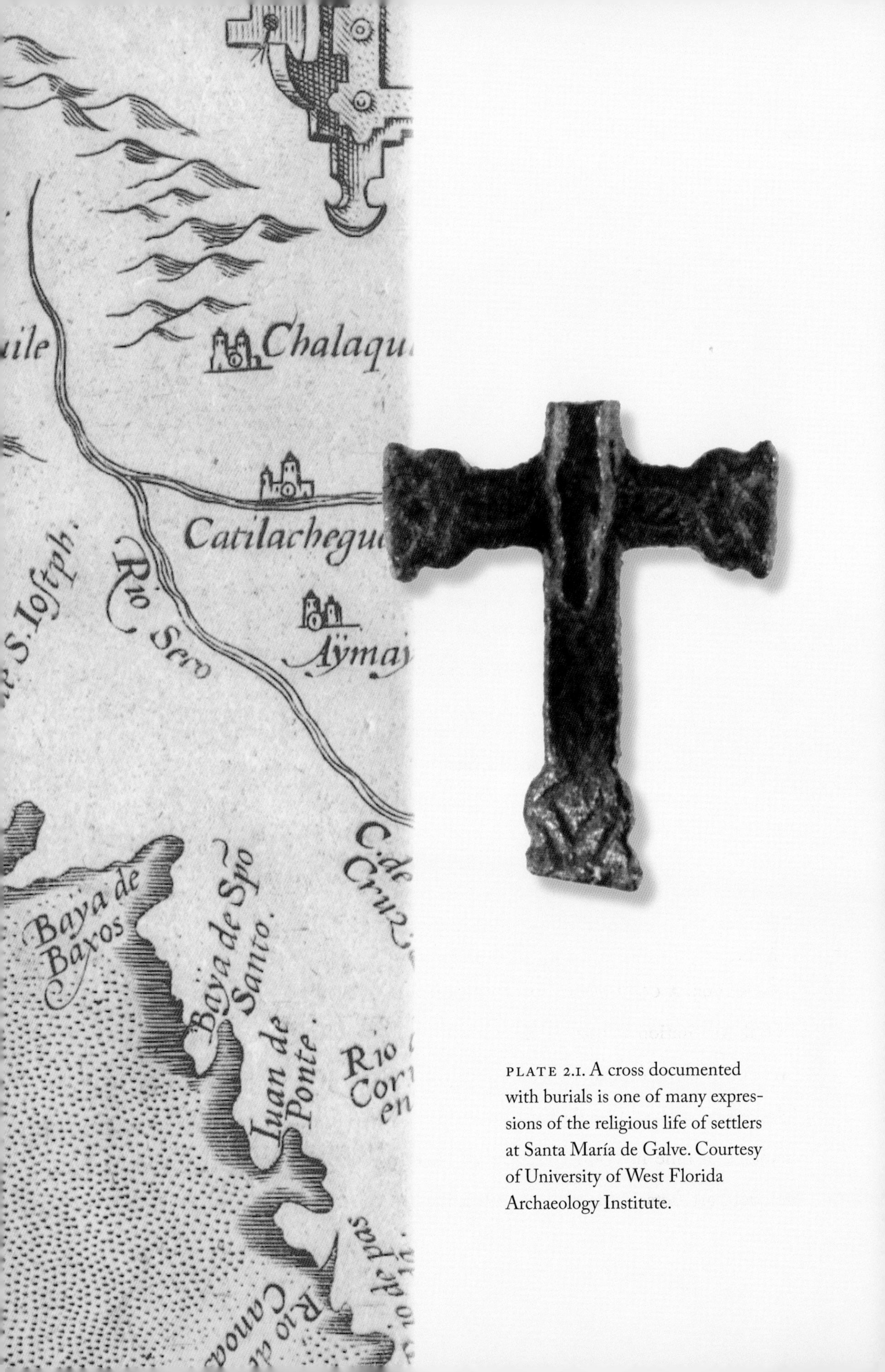

PLATE 2.1. A cross documented with burials is one of many expressions of the religious life of settlers at Santa María de Galve. Courtesy of University of West Florida Archaeology Institute.

TWO

First Pensacola
1698–1719

When all the large fleets in the world at present could anchor in any part of its length of nearly eleven leagues and width of one, two, and three and be protected from all winds, it is evident that this bay is most unusual.

—Carlos de Sigüenza y Góngora, royal cosmographer, to the Conde de Galve, viceroy of New Spain, June 1, 1693

In 1995, a construction crew digging a utility trench on Naval Air Station Pensacola, the sprawling 5,800-acre historic base to the west of modern Pensacola, inadvertently unearthed several human burials. University of West Florida archaeologists led by Judith Bense identified the remains of nine individuals, several of whom were buried with distinctive religious artifacts. Subsequent investigations revealed that this cemetery site was associated with a Spanish settlement founded in 1698, one known locally as First Pensacola.

Long after the Luna settlement had faded into memory, a diverse group of conscript soldiers and convict laborers built a second Spanish town at Pensacola. Known officially as Presidio Santa María de Galve, the fort and village complex was constructed atop the high bluffs overlooking the entrance to Pensacola Bay. The fort, named San Carlos de Austria after a European prince, was larger than a football field and built to ward off French and English threats to the Gulf Coast.

By the late seventeenth century, France had risen to a position of prominence in the Atlantic World. Under Louis XIV (1643–1715), the country emerged from decades of bloody religious civil war to chart a course of national consolidation and international expansion. Hardly cohesive by the standards of a modern nation-state, France was sufficiently unified to facilitate colonization efforts abroad. And colonize it did. By the late seventeenth century, the French empire of King Louis spanned the Atlantic to include colonial possessions in Canada and the Caribbean.

England, like France, had experienced decades of unification at home and expansion abroad to 1698. England was now a premier sea power and a very effective colonizer. From the founding of Jamestown in 1607 to that of South Carolina in 1670, the English tested Spanish claims to Florida. Conflict between England and France in King William's War (1689–1697)—a rather small-scale affair in the colonies but one with a European component—was

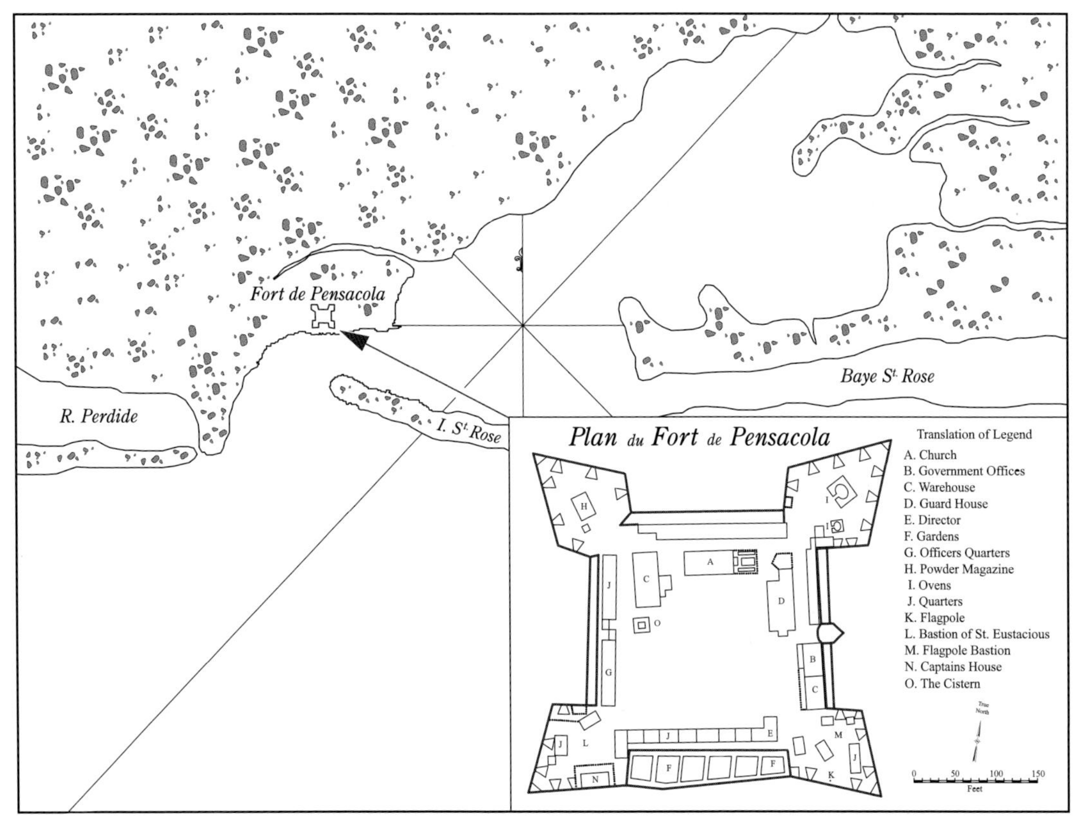

FIGURE 2.1. Design and location of Spanish fortifications established in 1698. Digitized and adapted from the photocopy of Carte del'Entre du Port, et Rade de Pensacola 1719. NL, Cartes Marines Edward E. Ayer Collection, Newberry Library, Chicago. Courtesy of University of West Florida Archaeology Institute.

all that prevented either of Spain's European rivals from colonizing peninsula Florida and the Gulf Coast.

English and French designs on the Gulf Coast were symptomatic of the decline of Spain's stature in the Atlantic World. The factors that coalesced to undermine the once mighty Spanish Empire were many and varied: an imbalanced, inefficient, and inflationary economy; ineffective and unbalanced rulers; and costly imperial wars. This lethal mix, combined with a decline in American silver imports, contributed to what is commonly known as Spain's Seventeenth-Century Crisis. By late century, the Spanish Empire appeared to be in danger of collapse, and nowhere was it more vulnerable than along the northern Gulf Coast. Although Spanish missions dotted the landscape from St. Augustine to the Apalachicola River, there were no Spanish settlements between the Apalachicola and the Trinity River in Texas. This vast unsettled region was proving irresistible to the English and the French, who coveted the vast unpopulated frontier of great strategic significance. The French threat was personified best by an ambitious French-Canadian named Rene Cavalier, Sieur de La Salle.

La Salle and the Rediscovery of Pensacola

With the northern Gulf Coast as his destination, Sieur de La Salle set sail from France in 1685, striking fear in the hearts of Spanish officials on both sides of the Atlantic. To that date, officials had dismissed French schemes in the region as idle threats. But the threat posed by La Salle was very real, and he had a resumé to prove it. The Frenchman had descended the Mississippi to its mouth in 1682 and claimed all the land drained by the great river for his king. In 1685, La Salle was returning to the Gulf Coast to make good on that claim. However, he overshot the mouth of the Mississippi by some 600 miles and founded an ill-fated settlement on Matagorda Bay, Texas. For our purposes, the real significance of La Salle lay in the many Spanish expeditions he inspired, one of which "rediscovered" Pensacola Bay in 1686.

Mexican officials first learned of the La Salle expedition in September 1685 from a young man by the name of Denis Thomas. Captured aboard a French privateer ship, Thomas disclosed that he had been part of an expedition bound for the Gulf Coast. When Thomas's testimony was corroborated with that of other French prisoners in Mexican jails, the search was on for what historian Robert Weddle calls the "French thorn." Between 1685 and 1690, eleven Spanish expeditions went in search of this thorn that threatened to infect the entire Gulf Coast. The expedition of Juan Enríquez Barroto and Antonio Romero rediscovered Pensacola Bay in 1686. Juan Jordán de Reina, a young ensign who accompanied Enríquez Barroto and Romero, kept a diary of the trip. Jordán recorded that Pensacola Bay was "the best I have ever seen" and that local natives called it Panzacola. A year later, Spanish naval officer Andrés de Pez made the first of his three voyages to the Gulf Coast in search of La Salle.[1] Although he never ventured into Pensacola Bay, Pez became enamored with the idea of a settlement on its shores, from which he might govern a vast new North American colony.

He proposed the settlement of the bay in what came to be known as the Pez Memorial. However, the 1689 document was not the handiwork of Pez but of the Mexican intellectual Carlos de Sigüenza y Góngora. In the memorial, Sigüenza embellished Pensacola with an abundance of wild fruits, wild game, stands of timber sufficient to outfit the nations of Europe with fleets, and the best natural harbor on the Gulf Coast. It was mostly true. There certainly were some wild fruits and game in the pine barrens around Pensacola Bay. Timber was obviously abundant. And the bay was an excellent natural harbor. Adopting Sigüenza's work as his own, Pez went to Spain to promote the idea of a Pensacola settlement. There, the king's counselors rebuked this "new Columbus," who claimed to have discovered what he had not and proposed to colonize what he had yet to explore. They belittled each of his proposals, pointing out that the French and the English already had visited the bay and that neither had shown an inclination to colonize it. Reluctant to abandon long-established colonies or to found new ones, the counselors recommended only naval patrols to keep foreign interlopers out.[2]

The Spanish king, Charles II (1661–1700), whose incessant bouts of mental illness earned him the nickname "the bewitched," typically participated little in the affairs of government. But on this occasion the troubled king gathered his senses, or so it seemed, just long enough to rebuff the advice of his counselors and proclaim his support for a colony at Pensacola Bay, but not for the abandonment of St. Augustine. All that stood in the way of Pez's dream of a North American colony centered on the bay was a requisite reconnaissance mission and scientific investigation of the area.

For this task, the Mexican Viceroy Conde de Galve turned to Carlos de Sigüenza, the author of the report that had stirred a despondent Spanish monarch to decisive action. Sigüenza was priest, scientist, mathematician, cartographer, linguist, engineer, historian, writer, poet, and antiquarian, but he was hardly an explorer. Until 1693, the Mexican scholar had never traveled more than a few hundred miles from his home in Mexico City.[3] Juan Jordán, who was making his second voyage to Pensacola Bay, accompanied the ambitious Pez and inexperienced Sigüenza.

Setting out from Veracruz, the Pez-Sigüenza expedition reached Pensacola on April 7, 1693. Once arrived, Sigüenza rechristened the bay Bahía Santa María de Galve in honor of the Virgin Mary and Mexican viceroy and proceeded to name the landforms and streams in the region. The western tip of the barrier island of Santa Rosa became Siguenza Point and the bluffs opposite the island, the Cliffs of St. Thomas. After two weeks, the expedition moved on to Mobile Bay and the mouth of the Mississippi River, but it was Pensacola Bay that captured Sigüenza's imagination. Back in Mexico, the

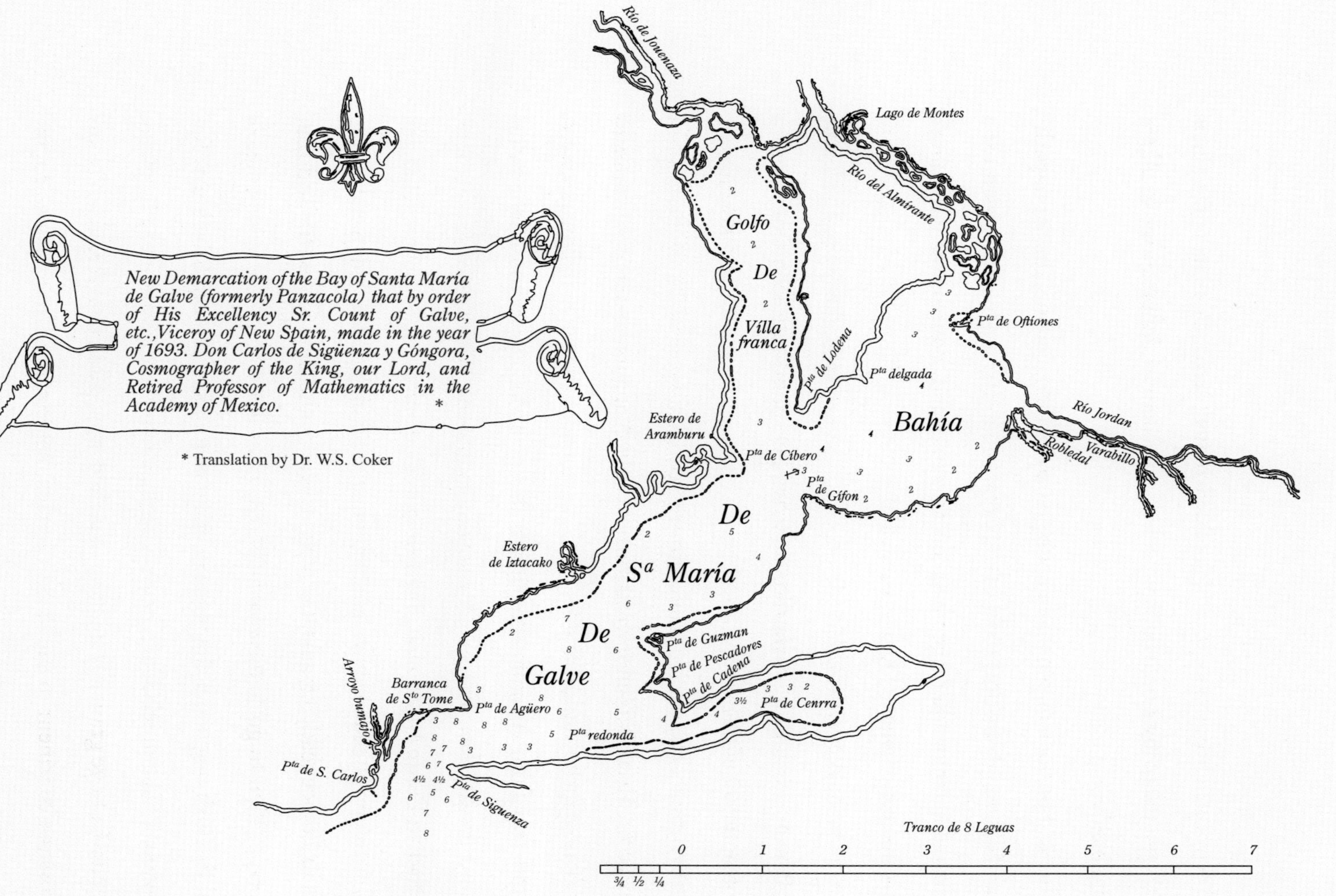

FIGURE 2.2. Pensacola Bay as mapped by Carlos de Sigüenza in 1693. Digitized adapted version. AGI Seville: Mexico, 61–6–21. Courtesy of University of West Florida Archaeology Institute.

old scholar's enthusiasm poured forth: "I hereby assert that bay is the finest jewel possessed by His Majesty . . . not only here in America but in all his kingdom."

In the summer of 1693, Pez returned to Spain to report on the expedition's findings. Skeptical counselors, expressing little more enthusiasm for a Pensacola venture than they had on Pez's first visit, nonetheless went along with the king's wishes. Three years passed, however, and nothing happened. The death of the Viceroy Conde de Galve and the court-martial of Andrés de Pez, on charges of cowardice and dereliction of duty stemming from a confrontation with French privateers off the coast of Cuba, delayed matters. Pez eventually cleared his name but missed his chance to be the founder of Pensacola. That distinction went to a decorated Spanish naval officer, Andrés de Arriola, who had won great acclaim three years earlier when he sailed round-trip from Acapulco to Manila in just under eleven months, a world record for his day.[4] For his Pensacola assignment, Arriola had the French-Canadian Pierre Le Moyne, Sieur d'Iberville to thank.

In the spring of 1697, a Spanish spy alerted officials in Madrid that Iberville was in France readying a fleet of ships to sail to the Gulf Coast. In outfitting an expedition to go to the coast, Iberville was not so much reacting to general Spanish neglect of the region as he was to a specific English threat. The previous year, Daniel Coxe, personal physician to the royal family in England, acquired a huge grant of land that stretched from modern Georgia westward across the continent to the Pacific. In this vast expanse Coxe planned to initially settle some 200 Huguenot families on 500,000 acres. And this was only the beginning. The Coxe grant threatened to drive a wedge between French colonies in Canada and potential new ones along the Gulf Coast.[5] Iberville intended to make sure that did not happen.

To counter the French drive to the coast, a new Mexican viceroy, José Sarmiento Valladares, the Conde de Moctezuma, turned to his most gifted naval officer, Andrés de Arriola. The record-setting sea captain had visited both Pensacola Bay and the mouth of the Mississippi River in the months following his round-trip voyage to Manila. Arriola argued vehemently that the rich Mississippi Delta floodplain, rather than the sterile Pensacola bayshore, was Iberville's destination, just as it had been La Salle's. Arriola's criticism of Pensacola Bay embroiled him in a controversy with Carlos de Sigüenza that lasted down to the old scholar's death in 1700, but it did not change his own fate: he was destined to be the founder—albeit a reluctant one—of Presidio Santa María de Galve.

In mid-October, about the time that Iberville departed France, Arriola sailed from Veracruz with some 350 men, bound for Pensacola Bay. In early November, Juan Jordán set out from Havana on his third voyage to the bay, accompanied by some fifty or sixty men. Jordán arrived first on November 17 and quickly set up camp on the western end of Santa Rosa Island, near Siguenza Point. Arriola followed four days later and immediately relocated the main camp from the low, swampy island environment to the Cliffs of St. Thomas (subsequently known simply as the Red Cliffs), high clay bluffs on the mainland opposite the point and the site of the modern-day Naval Air Station. The November landfall of Arriola and Jordán gave the Spanish a two-month head start on the French.[6]

Sieur d'Iberville reached Pensacola Bay in late January 1699 at the head of French forces of some 1,000 men. Reluctant to go ashore himself, Iberville sent a contingent that included his younger brother, Jean Baptiste, Sieur de Bienville. Little impressed by the Spanish forces assembled on the shores of Pensacola Bay on that winter day, which included a good number of pardoned convict laborers dressed up to look like soldiers, Bienville was nonetheless captivated by the bay they guarded: "tinsel that dazzles at first sight," the Frenchman recalled years later.[7]

Settlement

After the French forces departed, Arriola turned his attention to finishing the presidio he had begun in November. As in the sixteenth century, Spanish town planning mandated that the settlement be laid out on a grid pattern. Overseeing construction of the fort and village complex was Jayme Franck, an Austrian military engineer best known for his redesign of Fort San Juan de Ulloa, the mighty stone fortress that defended the harbor at Veracruz. A year and a half into his service at Pensacola, however, a sickly and dispirited Franck departed the bay, his work still unfinished. Back in Mexico, the once-proud engineer committed suicide. Responsibility for finishing and repairing the fort at Pensacola fell to a series of military engineers and officers with little or no engineering experience. And the need to maintain the fort in a defensible condition was becoming ever more important as the War of Spanish Succession heated up in the European theater and showed signs of spilling over onto the American frontier.

The death of the last Spanish Hapsburg king, Charles II, in 1700 sparked the War of the Spanish Succession (1702–1713), known as Queen Anne's War in America. It pitted England, Holland, and Austria against France and Spain. Through a dozen years of war, Philip of Anjou, nephew of King Louis XIV of France, maintained a French claim to the Spanish throne. For the Pensacola settlers, the war and the presence of a Bourbon prince—crowned King Philip V (1700–1746)—on the throne had two consequences: the Louisiana French became helpful allies and the Carolina English implacable enemies.

Initially, the Spanish believed that the French had abandoned their Gulf Coast venture in January 1699. However, Iberville had other plans. After encountering the Spanish at Pensacola Bay, he sailed west and founded the first capital of French Louisiana on Biloxi Bay at modern-day Ocean Springs, Mississippi. Arriola only stumbled upon the French settlement by chance in March 1700 while following up on rumors of English ships in the area. In a bold move, Iberville relocated his capital to Mobile in 1704, placing the French on the doorstep of Spanish Pensacola.

Settlers

Pensacola, at the time, hardly represented a threat to the French in the region. The population of the presidio generally fluctuated between 200 and 300 persons, although it increased to many times this number in times of war. Although consisting primarily of conscript soldiers and convict laborers, particularly in the early years, the population included military officers,

PLATE 2.2. Adapted stylized depiction of settlers at Santa María de Galve. Adapted after *A Description of the Kingdom of New Spain of 1774* (Yndio, y Mestizo, Cayote) by Pedro Alonso O'Crouley. Original manuscript in the Biblioteca Nacional, Madrid, Spain.

PLATE 2.3. Colonoware sherds recovered at Santa María de Galve with reproduction vessels. Reproductions by Robin Rodgers. Photograph by Al Audleman. Courtesy of University of West Florida Archaeology Institute.

government bureaucrats, priests, civilians, and Indians. The harsh, Florida frontier did not attract many civilian settlers, and the number of women and children in early Pensacola remained small. However, Hispanic and Indian families fleeing English-Creek raids on the Apalachee mission province did migrate to the town beginning in 1704. Historical evidence of the Apalachee migration is abundant, but archaeological evidence exists as well, in a distinctive pottery type called colonoware.

Colonoware is a handmade, low-fired pottery made from local clays that served as kitchenware in colonial households, particularly where more refined cooking and storage vessels were in short supply or where breakage was common. It exhibits a fusion of European, Indian, and/or African ceramic traditions. In the case of the colonoware found at Pensacola, it also exhibits design patterns suggestive of an Apalachee influence.[8]

That there are no other distinctive design patterns of colonoware in the archaeological record of the presidio is a testament to the earlier departure of local groups from the area. Initially, some Indians returned to the Spanish presidio for short visits, but in time these visits became less frequent. Native groups did not remain for any length of time, establishing a pattern that continued for most of the two decades of Spanish occupation. Even most of the Apalachee Indians arriving in 1704 soon moved on, enticed by French trade goods to the west. More than a decade passed before they returned to Pensacola.[9]

PLATE 2.4. Image of Our Lady of Guadalupe incorporating Old World Catholic and New World Aztec symbolism. Original in the Basilica of Guadalupe, Mexico City.

Women are rarely noted in the historical record of the presidio. However, glimpses of them are seen in the archaeological record, reflected in clothing fasteners, adornments, jewelry, and beads. Also, women took part in the religious life of the community, which would have incorporated the Virgin of Guadalupe. This Mexican virgin, possessing elements of the Aztec goddess Tonatzin and the Catholic Virgin Mary, stands atop a crescent moon supported by a dark-skinned angel, cloaked in a blue mantle covered with stars and surrounded by the sun. Archaeologists recovered a religious medal with an image of the Virgin of Guadalupe at the presidio. They also unearthed several cobalt blue glass beads with stars and a crescent moon beneath the church floor. Although similar to the Guadalupe imagery described above, they are of French origin. These artifacts vividly reflect the mixing of Old and New World beliefs and, undoubtedly, the participation of both sexes in the community's spiritual life.[10]

PLATE 2.6. Religious medallion recovered at Santa María de Galve depicting Our Lady of Guadalupe. Courtesy of University of West Florida Archaeology Institute.

PLATE 2.5. Man in the Moon beads with remnants of gold stars showing. Courtesy of University of West Florida Archaeology Institute.

The number of women and children at the presidio may have increased over time. However, there were many factors to discourage families from taking up residence on the shores of Pensacola Bay. These included food shortages, diseases, fires, Indian raids, and hurricanes.

Survival

Acute food shortages at Presidio Santa María de Galve stemmed from the same factors that haunted Luna's settlement, chief among them being the infertile sandy soils that stretched for miles around Pensacola Bay and made large-scale agriculture impossible. Colonists initially relied on the *situado*: a collection of rations, wages, munitions, bonuses, and household goods that originated in Veracruz and were sent periodically to Pensacola. However, the presidio soon turned to alternative sources to augment an irregular supply line.[11]

Down to 1713, trade flourished between the French in Mobile and the Spanish in Pensacola, although only a small percentage of trade items ever appeared on any books. The remainder might be termed illicit, or undocumented, trade. Evidence of this illicit trade might be best illustrated in the recovery of hundreds of sherds of Chinese porcelain recovered at the site of French Mobile and presumed to have come via trade with the Spanish from Pensacola, Havana, and Veracruz.[12] The presence of expensive porcelain at both Mobile and Pensacola suggests that these frontier outposts were linked

PLATE 2.7. Majolica cache recovered from a pit adjacent to the fort warehouse. Courtesy of University of West Florida Archaeology Institute.

to a worldwide network as well as to each other through undocumented trade.

As governor of a neglected settlement on a distant frontier, Gregorio de Salinas Varona (1711–1717) was the master of the illicit trade game along the Gulf Coast. According to François Le Maire, a visiting French priest at Pensacola, Salinas Varona was bad for business in Mobile: "The little money in circulation in our colony has come from Pensacola. . . . But two years ago, a new governor came to Pensacola. By means of a shop and warehouse filled with all kinds of merchandise he has cut all channels through which some part of this money could flow into our colony."[13] While the enterprising Salinas Varona was undermining trade that was essential to Mobile's survival as a colony, a number of factors were threatening Pensacola's future. These included disease, hurricanes, fires, and both European and indigenous enemies.

Diseases contributed to the deaths of hundreds, if not thousands, of presidio residents, but hurricanes brought their own form of destruction. One particularly well-documented hurricane occurred on September 3, 1705. On that day, Spanish naval officer Antonio de Landeche brought his ship, the *Nuestra Señora del Rosario y Santiago Apostol*, into Pensacola Bay and dropped anchor just north of Siguenza Point. There, he prepared to load the region's most valuable export: timber. Before Landeche could take on his cargo, however, a powerful hurricane began to move ashore. According to reports, the admiral's crew battled the storm for the better part of two days. They chopped down

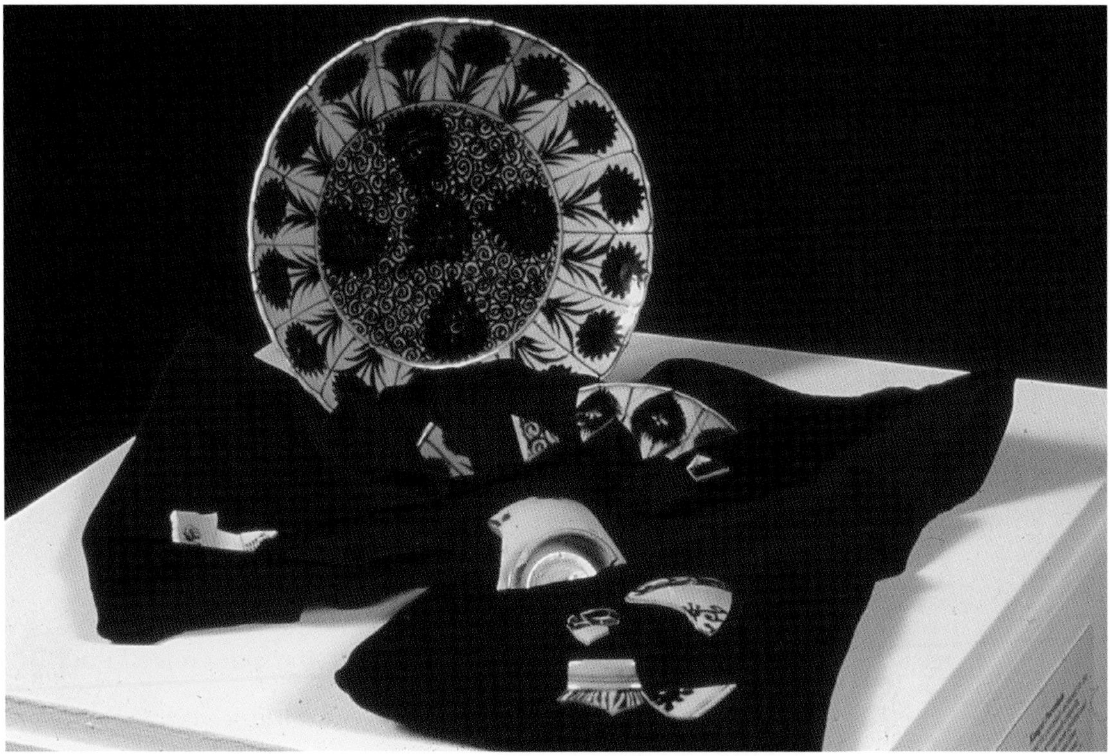

PLATE 2.8. Chinese (Kangxi period) porcelain sherds recovered at Santa María de Galve shown with an intact vessel from the Kangxi period (1662–1722) not associated with the site. Al Audleman photographer. Courtesy of University of West Florida Archaeology Institute.

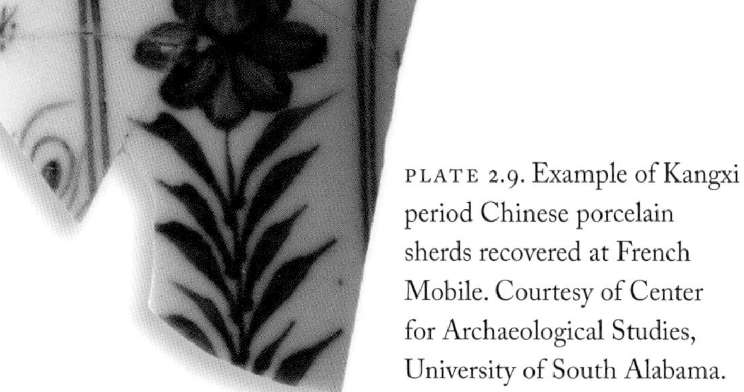

PLATE 2.9. Example of Kangxi period Chinese porcelain sherds recovered at French Mobile. Courtesy of Center for Archaeological Studies, University of South Alabama.

the ship's masts in an attempt to stabilize and save her. On September 5, late in the evening, the last of the *Rosario's* anchors gave way, and the ship surged toward Siguenza Point where it broke apart in the pounding surf. Landeche's ship was the victim of one of several hurricanes to strike Pensacola during the Spanish occupation of Presidio Santa María de Galve.[14]

In 1998, nautical archaeologists with the University of West Florida began excavating what appears to be the wreck of the *Rosario*. Because shipwrecks represent catastrophic events that seal a vessel and encapsulate its contents, they provide a treasure trove of date-specific information. The ceramics, glass, personal items, and animal bone recovered from the wreck, known officially as the Santa Rosa Island Ship, closely mirror artifacts and faunal remains recovered in excavations at the nearby Presidio Santa María de Galve. While hurricanes can produce a rich, time-specific archaeological record, fires can do much the same as they capture structures and their contents at one moment in time.

In the summer of 1707 Creek Indians, allies of the Carolinian English, attacked Presidio Santa María. They razed the village, laid siege to the fort, and initiated a series of raids that continued for the next half dozen years. Despite Creek assistance, the English were unable to wrest Florida from the Spanish. With the end of the War of Spanish Succession in 1713, Spanish-Creek relations improved on the frontier, as former enemies turned allies. The Creeks subsequently rebelled against the English in what came to be known as the Yamassee War (1715–1716). Spanish-French relations cooled over this same period.

PLATE 2.10. Assorted ship rigging and wood tools (including sheaves, rope, fiddle block, toggle, bilge scoop, and tool handle). Courtesy of University of West Florida Archaeology Institute.

The End of First Pensacola

After 1713, the Spanish and the French did not cooperate as they had. Even worse, these one-time allies became enemies in the War of the Quadruple Alliance (1718–1720). When England, Holland, Austria, and France took exception to Philip's revival of claims to the French throne that he had renounced in the Treaty of Utrecht in 1713, a war ensued. On January 9, 1719, France declared war on its neighbor across the Pyrenees, and on May 15 Bienville convinced an outmanned and unprepared Spanish garrison at Pensacola to surrender.

The Spanish returned to oust the French on August 6, 1719, and usher in a second, short-lived occupation of Pensacola; perhaps anticipating another loss, the Spanish may have taken measures to protect their assets from seizure by burying some of their artillery. Finally, on September 17 of the same year the French retook Pensacola for the final time and burned the fort and village to discourage the Spanish from returning. Thereafter, they left a small contingent of soldiers to guard the charred remains for the next two years. The end of the war brought status quo antebellum, meaning a return of Pensacola to Spain.[15] The charred remains of the fort walls in the archaeological record vividly mark the catastrophic fire, which led the Spanish to reassess their settlement options on Pensacola Bay.

PLATE 2.11. Exhibit of artifacts and botanical and faunal remains recovered from the *Rosario* including coarse earthenwares, deer bone, peach pits, corncob, pig bone, coffee beans, fish vertebrae, and fishing net weights. The weights suggest that by the early eighteenth century, utilization of the rich marine resources of the Gulf of Mexico and Pensacola Bay was well under way. Courtesy of University of West Florida Archaeology Institute.

Summary

Santa María de Galve's founding was a response to French and English designs on the Gulf Coast. Birthed in an age of imperial warfare and declining Spanish fortunes, attacked by European and Indian enemies, ravaged by fire, battered by storms, plagued by malnutrition and its related diseases, debilitated by severed supply lines and by an unmotivated and dispirited population of conscript soldiers and convict laborers, the presidio nonetheless held fast as a Spanish foothold on the northern Gulf Coast for two decades. In the end, Spain's inability to adequately populate and supply the distant frontier presidio made it vulnerable to the designs of European rivals.

The life of Juan Jordán de Reina parallels that of the Pensacola colony he helped found. He first sailed to Pensacola in 1686 with Juan Enríquez Barroto, then again with Andrés de Pez in 1693. In 1698, he made his final voyage with Andrés de Arriola. Overlooked for a position of leadership at Presidio Santa María de Galve, he died two years later a sickly and dispirited man on the shores of the bay that so captivated him. However, his dedication to Pensacola laid the permanent foundations of a rich Hispanic cultural tradition that persists to the present day.

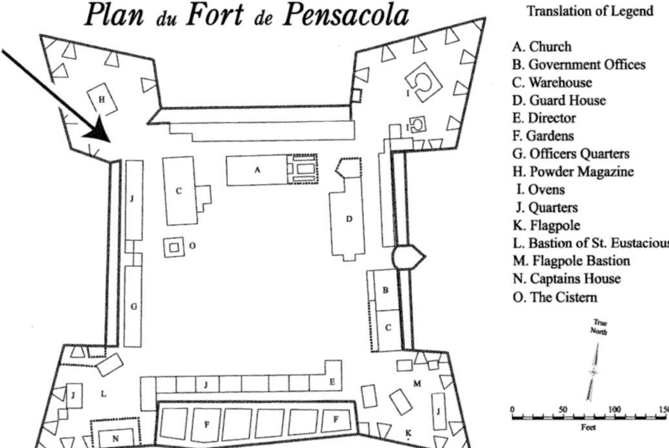

PLATE 2.12. Cannons in situ in the northwest bastion of Fort San Carlos de Austria with location in the fort pinpointed. Courtesy of University of West Florida Archaeology Institute.

RECIPE: Champurrado

Champurrado is a mixture of two important pre-Columbian ingredients: chocolate and corn *masa*. It is a nourishing and soothing drink, particularly on a cold night. Both the Maya and the Aztec treasured chocolate. In pre-Columbian America, the seeds, or "beans," of the cocoa tree were roasted, cooled, ground into a paste, formed into small cakes, and allowed to harden. In colonial times, chocolate was among the items sent to be administered to the sick, and such was the case in early Pensacola.

To prepare the beverage *chocoatl*, the cakes of chocolate were heated in boiling water with various spices or flavorings added—including vanilla pods, honey, and dried chiles. This mixture was beaten with a *molinillo* (carved wooden whisk) until frothy. The drink, consumed during certain religious rites, was considered an aphrodisiac as well as a ready source of quick energy. Spanish explorers brought chocolate back to Europe, and by the early seventeenth century it had become one of the most desired substances in both the Old and the New World: it remains so to the present day.

2 oz. (about ½ cup) *masa harina* (tortilla flour)
3 cups water
2 to 3-inch cinnamon stick
1 small split vanilla pod/bean
3 cups milk
3 oz. Mexican chocolate (or any unsweetened chocolate), grated
2 oz. *piloncillo* (raw sugar), or light brown sugar

Combine *masa harina* and water in a large saucepan. Using a whisk, whip and blend mixture until smooth. Add the cinnamon stick and the vanilla pod; cook and stir over medium-low heat until mixture has thickened.

Gradually stir in milk. Add the grated chocolate. Continue to cook until the chocolate has dissolved, beating constantly with a whisk or a *molinillo*. Inserted into the liquid and whirled between the palms of the hands, the *molinillo* creates a frothy texture.

When the chocolate mixture has become thick and creamy, discard the cinnamon stick and vanilla pod. Add sugar, beating well until all has dissolved. Pour into warmed cups and serve hot—background and recipe by Catherine Parker.

PLATE 3.1. Clay figurines recovered during excavations at Santa Rosa Pensacola. Courtesy of University of West Florida Archaeology Institute.

THREE

Storms and High Tides
1722–1763

> *The thirty-year history of this fort and this village, both called Santa Rosa Punta de Sigüenza, was told later in three words: Storms, high tides.*
>
> —Historian Stanley Faye

In the summers of 2003 and 2004, University of West Florida archaeologists excavating the site of Santa Rosa Punta de Sigüenza (1722–1757), the eighteenth-century Spanish presidio known locally as Santa Rosa Pensacola, unearthed several ceramic figurines in the shapes of humans and animals. Norma Harris, the archaeologist who oversaw the dig, theorizes that the figurines may have been associated with a church or a home altar in the tradition of Mexican-style Catholicism. This altar, along with everything else in the island presidio, had fallen victim to a November 1752 hurricane that forced the Spanish to once again reassess their settlement options on

Pensacola Bay. In doing so, they opted for the protected shelter of the bay interior, founding Presidio San Miguel de Panzacola (1757–1763) at the site of modern downtown Pensacola, which marked not only a new beginning but also the twilight of the Spanish era.[1]

Both Presidio Santa Rosa Pensacola and Presidio San Miguel de Panzacola came of age during a crucial period in the history of the Atlantic World. By the mid-eighteenth century, a struggle for supremacy—long waged between the Spanish, French, and English—was coming to a close. While France labored to maintain its colonies across the Atlantic, England positioned itself to become the dominant power in North America. Spain, like France, was simply no match for England.

In an age when wealth was built increasingly on commercial enterprise, Spain could not keep pace. The Iberian country continued to founder economically under the first Spanish Bourbon, Philip V, who was proving only slightly more stable than his Hapsburg predecessor, Charles II. In January 1724 Philip suddenly renounced the Spanish throne in favor of his sixteen-year-old son, Luis. When Luis died of smallpox in August, Philip returned to the throne but did little governing. For extended periods, he was precluded by recurring bouts of melancholy from signing any documents or enacting any policies, making him more a figurehead than an involved and decisive ruler. Granted, most Spanish kings played limited roles in policy making, but Philip played literally no role. It is doubtful if the Pensacola colony ever crossed his troubled mind.[2]

Return to Pensacola Bay

When the War of the Quadruple Alliance ended in 1721, Philip found himself once again in possession of Pensacola. Enthusiasm for this spoil of the peace table was short-lived. Fading in military might and struggling to pay for the defense of an unproductive frontier, Spain had to face reality: it no longer could afford the expensive liability that Pensacola had always been. In an effort to hold a defensive position at minimum cost to the Crown, Spanish officials searched for a cheap way to discourage its European rivals from settling the bay. They floated the idea of digging a canal across Santa Rosa Island to lower the depth of the water over the sandbar at the bay's entrance and thereby diminish its appeal. As an alternative to this whimsical plan that ran counter to the laws of physics, Spanish officials called for the settlement of the swampy, frequently inundated Siguenza Point on the western tip of Santa Rosa Island.[3]

Settlement

The task of reclaiming Pensacola fell to a Spanish naval officer of Scottish origin, Alejandro Wauchope. Reaching Pensacola in late November 1722, Wauchope found little to reclaim. Presidio Santa María de Galve, the fort and village complex constructed atop the high bluffs overlooking the entrance to the bay, was gone, the French having reduced it to little more than charred timbers. Wauchope dismissed outright the notion of digging a canal across the island. As to the idea of fortifying Siguenza Point, he criticized that location as "a low spot of extremely loose sand, full of marshes." Wauchope recommended a better site about a half mile east of the point where there were stands of pine trees, sand dunes, and fresh water springs. From a military standpoint, the site was strategic in its close proximity to the entrance to the bay. There, in December 1722, the first governor of Santa Rosa Pensacola began the new presidio on the shifting sands of a barrier island.

By building on the barrier island, the Spanish lessened the threat of an overland Indian attack and could better monitor the ship channel for any signs of European encroachment. However, they exposed themselves to a menace more destructive than Indians or European enemies: the tropical hurricane. Hurricanes, as the Luna colonists learned more than a century before, gave little more forewarning than an approaching enemy, and they could prove far more lethal to life and property. A major storm struck in September 1740 that all but destroyed the island town.

The reconstructed island settlement was the subject of a drawing by Dominic Serres. A French-born mariner working out of Havana, Cuba, Serres came to Pensacola in 1743 to sell goods along the coast. During his stay, this twenty-four-year-old aspiring artist with no formal training sketched a panoramic view of the Spanish presidio on Santa Rosa Island. Captured aboard a Spanish ship by British forces in 1745, during the War of the Austrian Succession (1740–1748)—King George's War in the colonies (1744–1748)—

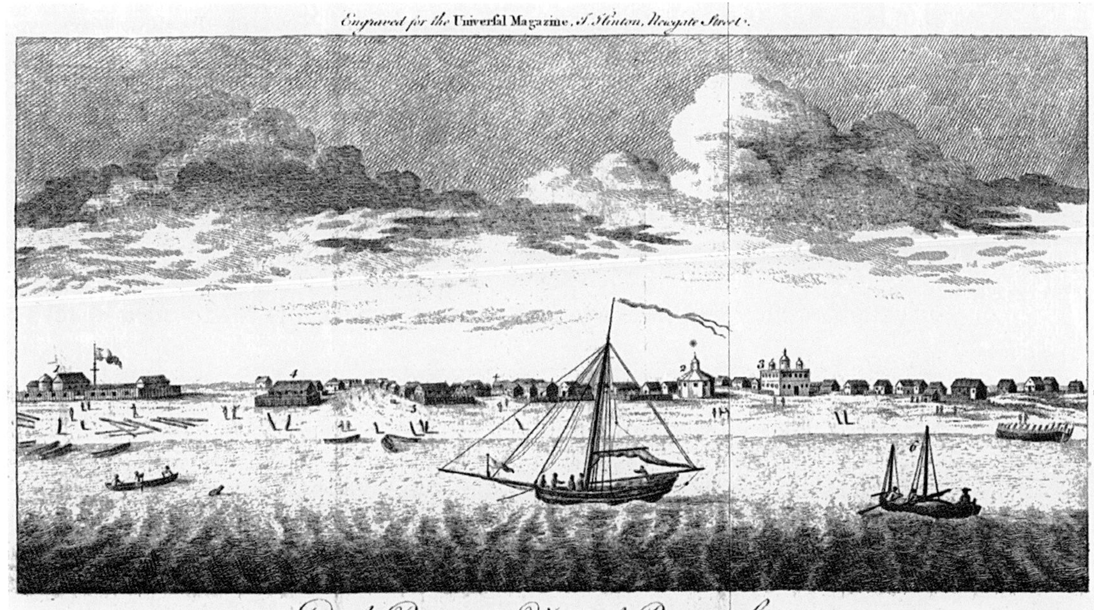

Engraved for the Universal Magazine, J. Hinton, Newgate Street.
A Perspective View of Pensacola.
1 The Fort. 2 The Church. 3 The Governors House. 4 The Commandants House. 5 A Well. 6 A Bungo.

FIGURE 3.1. *A Perspective View of Pensacola*. Drawn in 1743 and published in London in 1764, Dominic Serres's serene portrayal of Pensacola was utilized to entice British settlers to West Florida. *Universal Magazine*, 34 (January 1764). Copy on file at John C. Pace Library, Special Collections, University of West Florida, Pensacola.

Serres spent time in an English jail. Upon his release, the French expatriate remained in England, assimilated into London society, and raised a family. In time, he became a prominent painter of seascapes for King George III, but he maintained his love for landscapes. Somehow, his early sketch of Pensacola survived, and it appeared as "A Perspective View of Pensacola" in a 1764 English magazine.[4]

Serres's drawing of Santa Rosa Pensacola and a later Dutch revision provide historians and archaeologists with clues to the physical layout and architectural styles of the island presidio. The three buildings that dominate the settlement—the commandant's house, the governor's house, and the church—are more sophisticated in style and larger in size than the simple Caribbean-style structures prevalent throughout the town. While Serres's depiction of the island presidio is suggestive of what the town might have looked like (allowing for some artistic license) and also of its spatial organization (in that the panorama hints at a modified version of the grid pattern favored by Spaniards), the foreground of the sketch is instructive as well, hinting at the diversity of the maritime culture and economy in Pensacola. There are rowboats or canoes, small coastal sailing vessels, and a barge just offshore. The smaller vessels likely were involved in ferrying soldiers and civilians to and from the mainland to hunt and farm. The sailing vessel to the right of the drawing, known as a "bungo," probably took part in coastal trade. Original to Central America, where the hull was constructed from the trunk of a Guanacaste tree, the bungo was a common sight in Gulf waters during the colonial period and illustrates the spread of New World shipbuilding techniques throughout the Caribbean Basin. The barge in the picture probably functioned as a cargo ship, carrying supplies to Pensacola from Veracruz and Havana and taking timber out. The inclusion of Serres's drawing in a 1764 English publication was meant to entice settlers to the Gulf Coast. However, by this date the island presidio was but a memory, having been destroyed a dozen years earlier by yet another hurricane.

Settlers on a Formidable Frontier: High Tides, Illicit Trade, and a Strong Will to Survive

On November 3, 1752, a powerful storm struck Santa Rosa Pensacola. High winds pushed tidal surges over the island, washing away protective dunes, inundating sand streets, destroying virtually every building in town, and scattering survivors about the bay. The precise death toll is unknown, but generally the population of soldiers and civilians, with small numbers of convict laborers and Indians in the mix, averaged about 300. In the aftermath of the storm, officials counted fewer than 100 souls, but with island residents scattered among the farms (or *haciendas*) of the interior any population count was speculative at best.[5]

Despite the presence of working farms in the upper reaches of the bay, presidio residents found little in the way of food in the storm's aftermath and quickly turned to the French at Mobile and Dauphin Island to alleviate their sufferings. The French were more than happy to oblige their Spanish neighbors. It was in fact company policy—that of the French Company of the Indies that ran the Louisiana colony at the time—to aid the Pensacola Spanish as a way of fostering the only trade that could turn an unprofitable Louisiana enterprise into a profitable one.

Except in times of emergency, the Spanish Crown prohibited trade with the French. Royal decrees coinciding with the founding of Santa Rosa Pensacola not only banned this trade but meted out harsh punishments for offenders.

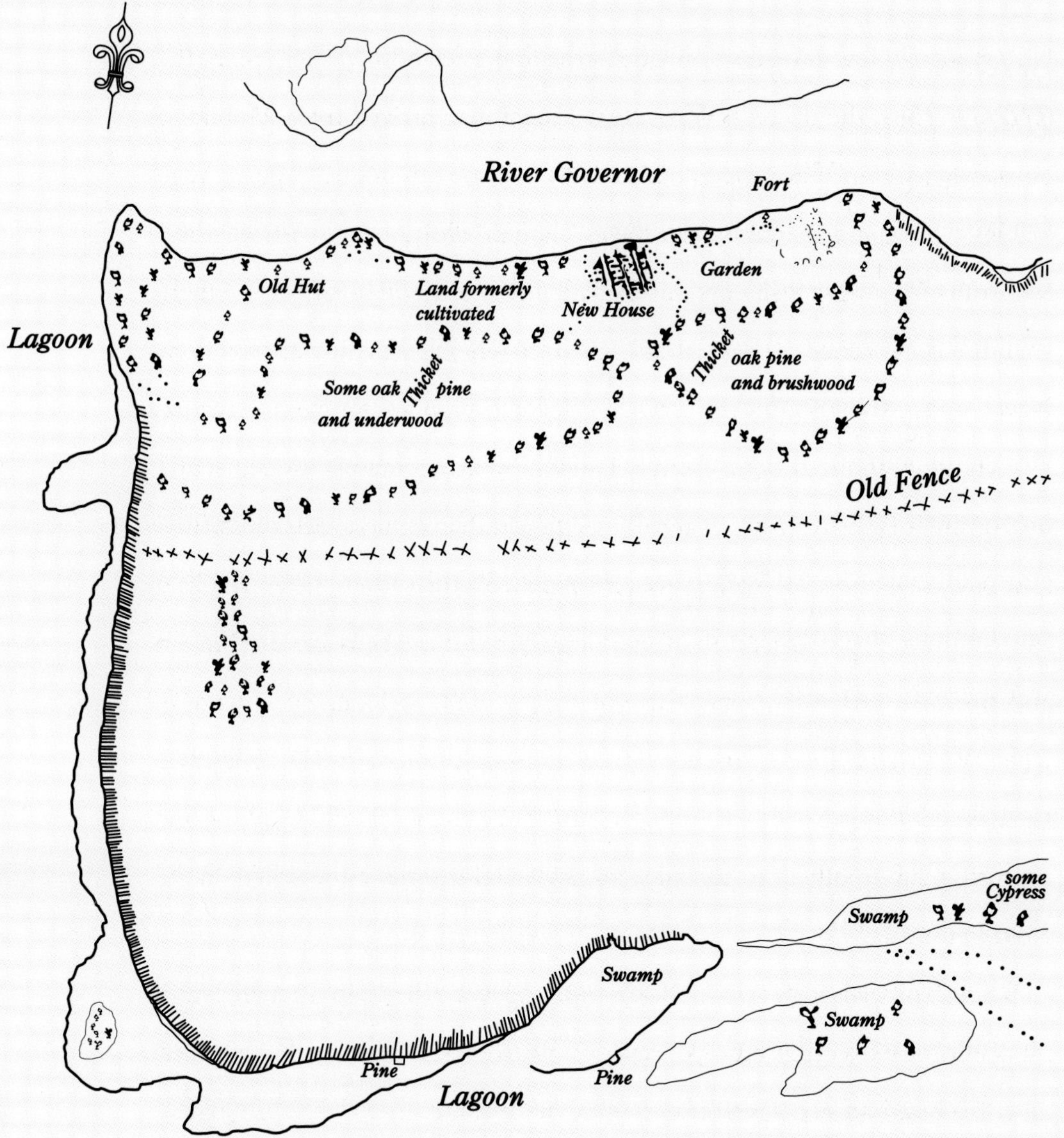

FIGURE 3.2. Survey showing an abandoned Spanish plantation on Escambia Bay at the time of British occupation ca. 1764. Digitized and adapted. Public Records Office of Great Britain, Kew, England. Class Five Files [CO5/604]. Manuscript on microfilm at John C. Pace Library, Special Collections, University of West Florida, Pensacola.

Unfortunately, few governors outside of the first, Alejandro Wauchope, bothered to enforce the decrees. When two Frenchman arrived from Mobile to Pensacola early in Wauchope's tenure with a canoe full of ducks, geese, vegetables, fruits, and merchandise, the Scotsman allowed them to sell their foodstuffs to hungry residents but forbade them to trade in any of the merchandise they carried. When other French traders subsequently arrived from New Orleans shortly after the arrival of Spanish supply ships from Veracruz, Wauchope prohibited them from even coming ashore and stationed sentinels on the beach to ensure that no presidio resident traded with them. This first governor of Santa Rosa Pensacola repelled other attempts as well in a vain attempt to put an end to all undocumented trade between the French and Spanish. His successors were not only willing to look the other way when it came to illicit trade but also anxious to profit from the enterprise themselves. This is hardly surprising, as smuggling represented one of the few incentives for an officer to remain in a neglected frontier outpost like Santa Rosa Pensacola.[6]

Spanish officials in Mexico and Madrid, long concerned with French smuggling efforts and a creeping westward expansion—New Orleans was founded in 1718—faced an even greater threat in the English. The Carolina English pushed continuously southward and by 1733 had founded the Georgia colony. With the English rapidly populating Georgia, there seemed to be a storm brewing on the doorstep of Spanish Florida, one that was destined to release its fury and vanquish all Iberian claims in the region.

The Spanish were helpless in the face of English expansion, as the Iberians had yet to right an empire that had nearly collapsed in the long and troubling seventeenth century. Ferdinand VI (1746–1759), the third Bourbon to sit on the throne in Spain, was proving no more competent than his troubled father, Philip V. He refused to sign any documents or enact any policies, meaning that the Spanish empire was virtually without any semblance of a ruler until Ferdinand's death in 1759. The Pensacola Spanish, however, were little concerned with affairs at court in Madrid as they were busy trying to rebuild their lives on a frontier ravaged by the devastating 1752 storm.

Move to the Mainland Settlement of Presidio San Miguel

In the immediate aftermath of the 1752 hurricane, officials in Mexico debated whether to abandon the island presidio or rebuild it. In the half dozen years following the hurricane, island residents began to congregate on the mainland between two freshwater streams, on a broad expanse of relatively flat land with good elevation: the site of modern downtown Pensacola. To 1752, there had been little more than a couple of buildings (possibly a blockhouse for soldiers and a mission for priests) in that location. Reports of a "great fort of stakes" there in 1753 appear to have been premature. Initial plans did call for a substantial fort of brick, but the military engineer in charge of construction, Philipe Feringan, began a much more modest wooden fort in 1757.[7]

That same year, the newly arrived Spanish governor, Miguel Román (1756–1761) christened the new settlement Presidio San Miguel de Panzacola to commemorate St. Michael the Archangel and the native peoples who once congregated around the bay. Despite its lofty name, San Miguel was unimpressive by almost any criteria. The fort, like its predecessors at Santa María de Galve and Santa Rosa Pensacola, was supposed to be the physical embodiment of Spanish power, but it was often falling in on itself. Nonetheless, within its feeble walls were a governor's house, chapel, assorted military buildings, and small houses. Outside the fort walls were some two-dozen houses, situated along the shoreline so as to take advantage of the sea breezes and allow for easy access into the fort via its east and west gates.

In constructing the new settlement, the Spanish paid heed to the long-established ordinances that governed town planning; however, they incorporated the formal elements in an informal arrangement, one possibly designed for maximum protection. At the center of the settlement was Feringan's fort, which suffered considerable damage in an August 1760 hurricane and stood as a sad testament to the efforts of the engineer. But the fort was defensible, and that was especially significant in the spring and summer of 1761 when Creek Indians attacked the town. To the Pensacola Spanish, the Indian raids appeared to be connected to the French and Indian War raging to the north.

The French and Indian War (1754–1760), known as the Seven Years' War in the European theater, was the culmination of nearly a century of conflict

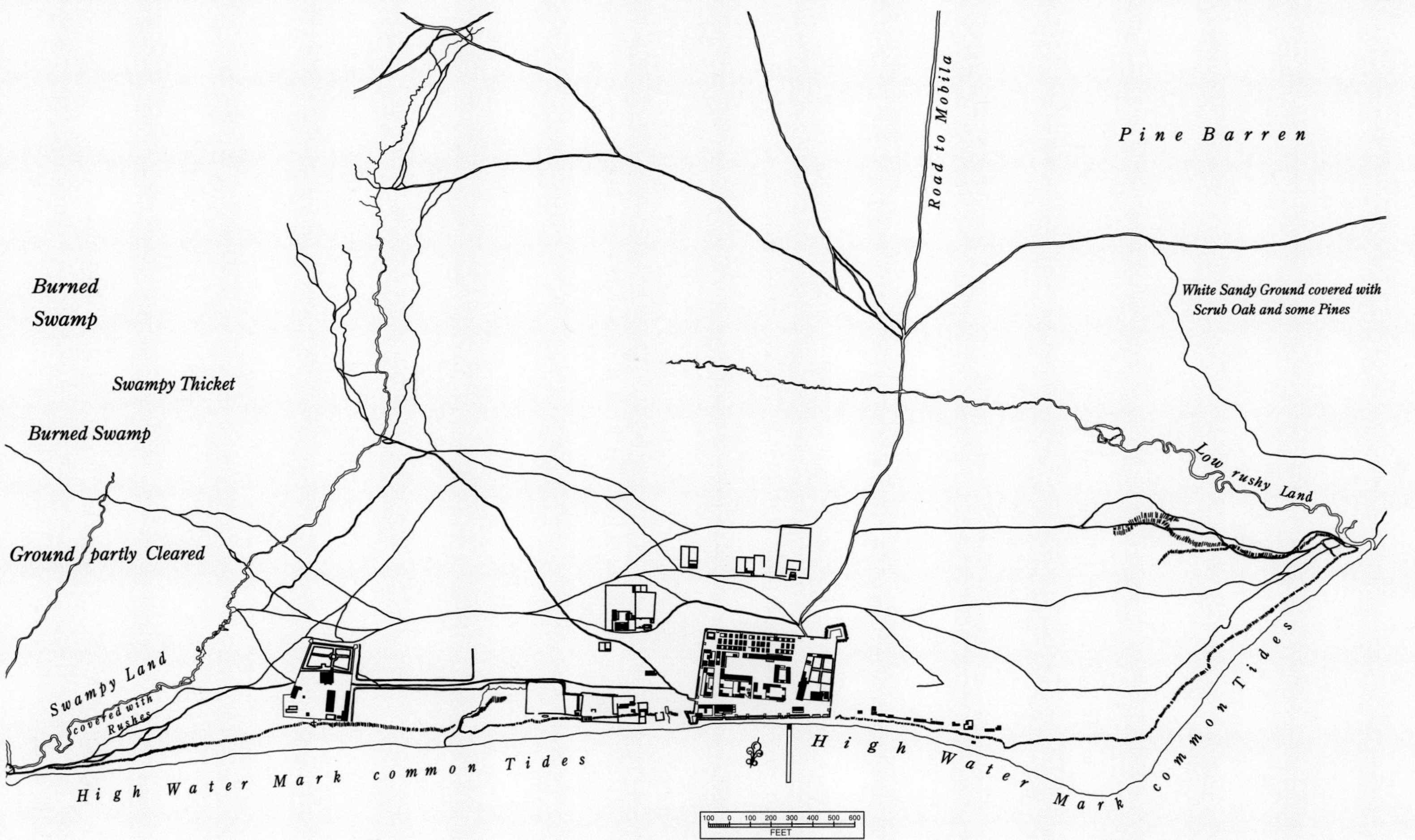

FIGURE 3.3. Compilation map of 1763 Pensacola. Digitized and adapted from photographic reproduction of PRO Co 700 Florida No. 20, London (town) and photocopy of PRO Co 700 No. 5, London (fort). Courtesy of University of West Florida Archaeology Institute.

between England and France. For well over a century, the two European rivals had been battling for supremacy in North America. The war proved a watershed event in this struggle. Previous conflicts in North America—King William's War (1689–1697), Queen Anne's War (1702–1748)—had been too limited in scope to bring about a decisive settlement. The French and Indian War, however, brought the long struggle to a head and, in doing so, changed the course of Pensacola's history, along with the rest of American history.

By the 1750s, it was apparent that the French had little prospect of holding back the tide of English expansion. The number of English colonists living along the Atlantic Seaboard was approaching two million, dwarfing the combined population of French and Spanish colonists living in North America. Moreover, the southern-most English colonies, South Carolina and Georgia, were the fastest growing of all, with thousands of settlers pushing southward and westward, threatening Spanish Florida as well as French Louisiana.

The Pensacola Spanish certainly felt threatened by the English and their Indian allies. Creek Indian raids on Presidio San Miguel in the spring and summer of 1761 were contemporary with the French and Indian War but appear to have been only indirectly related to the war itself. The raids were, nevertheless, violent and costly episodes in the history of early Pensacola. In the fall of 1761 Creeks targeted villages of Spanish-allied Indians living near the town, killing men, women, and children. In the late spring and early summer of 1761, they raided San Miguel itself, leaving several dead and wounded. With the help of their old allies, the French, the Spanish forged a peace with the Creeks but not before more than 100 combatants and innocents had died on both sides.[8]

Creek attacks on Presidio San Miguel can be seen in the archaeological record. In 1997, archaeologists with the University of West Florida unearthed evidence of these beneath the wooden floors of Old Christ (Episcopal) Church. Located in the heart of the colonial historic district, Old Christ Church dates to 1832, making it the oldest Protestant church on its original site in Florida. Situated a short distance from what would have been the eastern wall of the Spanish fort San Miguel, the church contains crypts of nineteenth-century rectors buried beneath its floors.[9] But beneath the rectors are an undisturbed colonial land surface and the charred foundations of an eighteenth-century Spanish structure.

Historical documents reveal that in the midst of Creek attacks in the summer of 1761, Spanish Governor Miguel Román ordered the destruction of houses that either posed a fire hazard to the fort or stood in the way of cannon and musket fire. Using cannons, Román leveled the buildings in the immediate vicinity of the fort and burned those at a greater distance. Archaeologist Elizabeth Benchley, who has researched the fort extensively, theorizes that the charred foundations beneath the floor of Old Christ Church belong to one of the buildings that the governor ordered burned in 1761.[10]

As the war wound down, Miguel Román found himself out of a job, as Diego Ortíz Parilla (1761–1763), a renowned Indian fighter from the Southwest, arrived in the late summer of 1761 to take control of the presidio. As

PLATE 3.2. Old Christ Church in downtown Pensacola. From the collection of West Florida Historic Preservation, Inc.

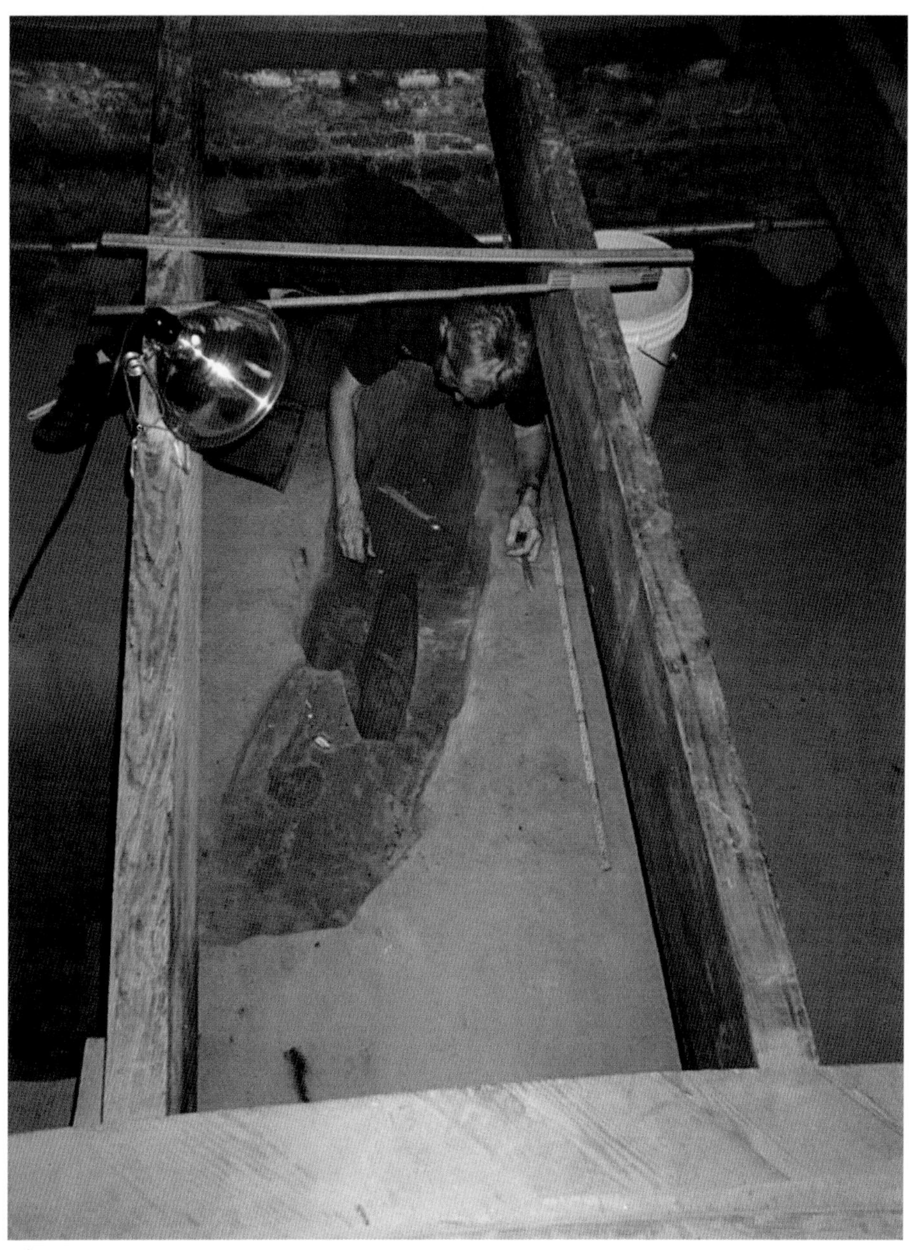

PLATE 3.3. Foundation trenches with burned timbers ca. 1761 excavated under the floor of Old Christ Church. Courtesy of University of West Florida Archaeology Institute.

required, the new governor conducted an obligatory review of his predecessor's tenure in office. Román did not fare well under the scrutiny of an investigation. Ortíz Parilla brought numerous charges of corruption and smuggling, but none stuck. With the investigation dragging on and town residents divided into separate camps, Pensacola was proving a valuable pawn at the peace tables of Paris.

In the latter stages of the French and Indian War, the conflict turned in favor of the English, to the detriment of not only the French but also the Spanish. As England's fortunes turned, Spain entered the war on the side of France. The Bourbon Family Compact of 1761, a wartime alliance between the French and Spanish royal families, brought nothing but heartache to Spain. In the course of the war, the English captured Havana, the port city through which the wealth of the New World flowed. With losses mounting and victory out of reach, the French and Spanish sued for peace.

Louis XV of France compensated his Spanish cousin Charles III (1759–1788) for his loyalty in the conflict before making peace with King George III of England. In November 1762, Louis transferred all of Louisiana west of the Mississippi River and New Orleans to Charles in the secret Treaty of Fontainebleau. The French king fully expected that his Spanish cousin would deal Louisiana and New Orleans to the English in order to secure the return of Havana. Charles, however, had no intention of giving the English a foothold so close to the silver mines of northern Mexico. As France ceded to England all of Canada and all of Louisiana east of Mississippi in the Treaty of Paris (1763), Spain relinquished Florida in return for Havana. In the exchange, the English gave up a valuable port city but acquired a long sought after port on the Gulf Coast.

With the arrival of the British military and settlers in Pensacola, Spanish residents left en masse, boarding ships for Veracruz and Havana. Included among the 800 or so departing in 1763 were approximately 100 Yamassee and Apalachee Indians and a contingent of free blacks. These Indians and free blacks went on to found the town of San Carlos in the state of Veracruz, later dispersing to settle other areas, including the village of Coyolillo. Today, residents of the small, remote village are a mixture of African and Indian blood. Most of these Afro-mestizos are farmers, cultivating corn, beans, squash, and chili peppers. Others work as craftsmen in the village. Still others serve as day laborers in neighboring towns and cities.

Coyolillo residents have remained closely tied to their village, fostering a strong oral history tradition. University of Veracruz anthropologist Sagario Cruz-Carretero has used this rich oral tradition and historical documents to trace some of Coyolillo's population of small farmers, craftsmen, and day laborers back to those who left Pensacola in 1763.[11] These individuals are legacies of the cultural exchanges in the colonial Caribbean Basin and are living links to the port city's vibrant Hispanic and African heritage.

PLATE 3.4. A typical house in Coyolillo, Mexico (note image of Our Lady of Guadalupe on the wall by the front door). Margo Stringfield collection.

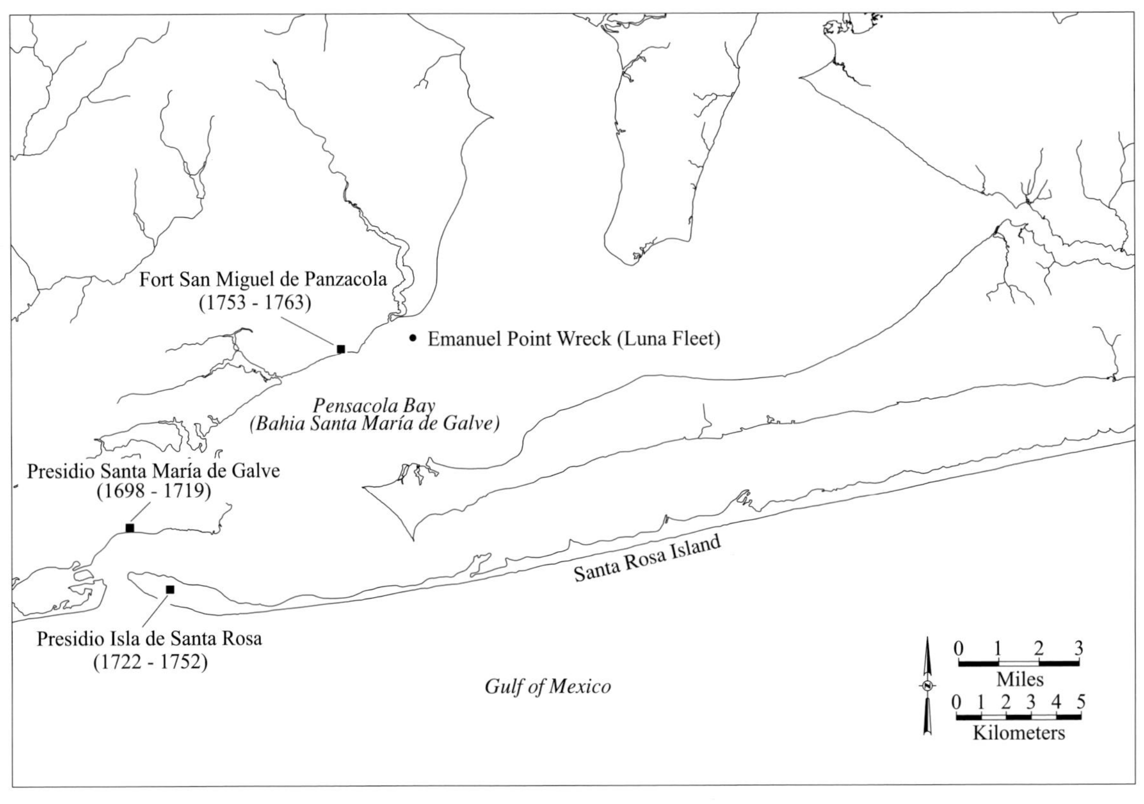

FIGURE 3.4. Map showing locations of Spanish settlements in Pensacola Bay from 1559 (Emanuel Point ships) to 1763. Digitized map courtesy of University of West Florida Archaeology Institute.

Summary

The early phase of Pensacola's Spanish history, referred to as its First Spanish Period, came to an abrupt end with the arrival of the English in 1763. To that year, the Spanish had occupied Pensacola Bay for over a half century with one brief interval of French occupation. But many of those departing in 1763 had been born in Pensacola. These natives were bound for places they had heard about but never seen, and the great majority would never return to the bay that they called home. They left behind relatively little to mark decades of occupation there. All that remains of Santa Rosa Pensacola and San Miguel are the decomposed foundations of their long destroyed structures and associated artifacts.

The history of Pensacola's First Spanish Period continues to be unraveled. Historians and archaeologists remain dedicated to telling the stories that are hidden in archives, buried beneath sands, and scattered on the floor of the bay. The Emanuel Point ships and the presidios of Santa María de Galve, Santa Rosa Pensacola, and San Miguel are tangible reminders of an age when this neglected outpost was at the center of the struggle for empire in the Atlantic World. They are also representative of the vibrant cultural exchanges that occurred among the peoples of the Caribbean Basin. This exchange, perhaps, is exhibited best in the melding of Old and New World religious practices, material culture, and foodways.

RECIPE: *Cocido Español*

Cocido Español is a meat and vegetable stew, the quintessential one-pot meal known in cultures all over the world. In Spain these stews are known as *cocidos*; the ingredients are locally produced and vary from region to region. They were—and still are—served in homes and in the better wayside inns and taverns throughout the countryside. The following recipe is similar to the stews of Castile, which was the home of many early explorers and soldiers who ventured to the New World and incorporates New World cultigens—tomatoes. Traditionally, a *cocido* is served as three separate courses: first, the broth; followed by the vegetables and legumes; and last, the meat.

1 pound dried chickpeas (garbanzos)
1 leek, washed and cut into large pieces
18 cups water
4 carrots, cut in large pieces
2 pounds flank or boneless chuck steak
3 cloves garlic, minced and crushed
1 beef soup bone
3 tomatoes, peeled and seeded
1 ham bone (if available)
4 medium potatoes, quartered
1 3–4 lb. chicken cut into large pieces
1 bay leaf
¼ lb. slab bacon cut into large pieces
2–3 whole cloves
1 lb. Spanish *chorizo** sausages
1 or 2 large onions, peeled and quartered
4–6 oz. fine noodles, cooked (optional)
Salt and pepper to taste

The day before serving: in a very large pot, put all the meats, except the *chorizos*, in eighteen cups of salted water. Bring to a boil; skim off any foam as it rises to the top. Simmer for one and one-half hours. Allow to cool, then refrigerate overnight. Put chickpeas to soak overnight in plenty of water to cover them.

Next morning, prepare the vegetables. Stick the whole cloves and bay leaf into sections of onion. Skim off all fat from top of broth. Return pot to stovetop; add all the vegetables and the *chorizo* sausages. *Be certain to use Spanish-style *chorizos* for best, authentic flavor.

Drain the chickpeas and add them to the large pot of meat and vegetables. Bring mixture to a gentle simmer, correct the seasoning, and cook—partially covered—for one hour (or longer, if desired). If noodles are to be used, cook them near the end of this time.

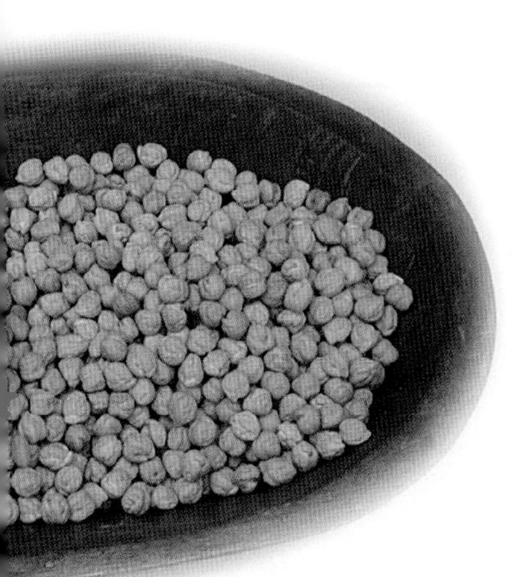

To serve in the traditional manner: divide broth into eight soup bowls; add portion of noodles to each, if desired. Serve hot as a first course. Cut meats into serving-sized pieces and arrange on a warm platter. Separate vegetables (according to type) and chickpeas on a second platter; serve alongside the meat, or keep warm and serve after the meat course.

For simpler service: divide broth into eight large soup plates; omit noodles. Have each person add his or her choice of meats, chickpeas, and vegetables to the hot broth and eat as a "one-dish" meal—background and recipe by Catherine Parker.

PLATE 4.1. Dice recovered from the Commanding Officers' Compound of the Fort of Pensacola. Courtesy of University of West Florida Archaeology Institute.

FOUR

British Pensacola
1763–1781

> *The British had a self-confidence bred by a century and a half of establishing initially profitless colonies and then making them pay. And that undertaking—not uplifting natives, nor cutting an imperial dash in bright uniforms, nor subjugating alien peoples—was the prime purpose of Britain's American empire in the 1760s.*
>
> —Historian Robin Fabel, *The Economy of British West Florida*

No historic structures stand in testament to the eighteen years that the British occupied Pensacola (1763–1781) or to the ingenuity of the astute urban planner Elias Durnford who laid the foundations of the modern town. However, beneath the streets, sidewalks, and parks of the historic downtown are the remnants of the old British town that Durnford designed. Visitors to Historic Pensacola Village can get glimpses of these remnants along the Colonial Archaeology Trail, a self-guided tour that meanders over the site of the old British fort.[1] Dice excavated from the site illustrate the mind-set of the British soldiers and settlers who cast their luck on the northern Gulf Coast in the aftermath of the French and Indian War.

The 1763 Treaty of Paris, which brought an official end to the Seven Years' War, forever changed the political landscape of North America and altered the struggle for supremacy in the Atlantic World and the Gulf region. The treaty, which altogether vanquished France from North America and eliminated the Spanish from Florida, is a testament to England's rise to prominence and to the corresponding decline of France and Spain. As Spain loosened its grip on a colony it had claimed since 1513, ministers in the court of Charles III—one of the so-called enlightened despots of the eighteenth century and the most effective ruler to sit on the Spanish throne in more than a century—endeavored to reform the empire. Charles preferred hunting to governing but managed to choose competent ministers who made for good government.

Unfortunately, Charles's French cousin Louis XV proved far less discerning in this area. Louis's indiscretion in the choice of ministers manifested itself in corrupt government, costly imperial wars, a deteriorating economy, and the loss of long-established colonies. Shorn of all of its North American possessions, the French empire in the Americas had shrunk to a few small sugar islands in the Caribbean. Years passed before the French or Spanish had a chance to avenge the losses suffered at the hands of the British in 1763. They would get that opportunity in the midst of the American Revolution at Yorktown, Mobile, and Pensacola, once again changing the balance of power in the Atlantic World.

The British Empire in America was never more extensive than it was in the years following the Seven Years' War. Within a couple of decades, the empire came unraveled, but in the immediate aftermath of the Treaty of Paris it encompassed vast stretches of the St. Lawrence and Mississippi River valleys, the Florida peninsula, and the Panhandle. The Proclamation Line of 1763, designed to prevent British colonists in the Atlantic Seaboard colonies from venturing westward onto Indian lands, also fixed the boundaries of Florida. In the Proclamation, the British carved two separate colonies out of the former Spanish possession. East Florida stretched from the Atlantic to the Apalachicola and Chattahoochee rivers, West Florida from the Apalachicola/Chattahoochee over to the Mississippi.

Settlers

British subjects flocked to the new, expansive colony with land speculators being the first to arrive in the summer of 1763. Acting on behalf of a consortium of investors, men like James Noble secured large land grants from the departing Spanish, many of which were later invalidated over the legality of

PLAN of the HARBOUR and SETTLEMENT of PENSACOLA
WEST FLORIDA
LOUISIANA
GULF OF MEXICO
Mouths of the Missisipi
BAY OF APALACHE
PENSACOLA
BAY OF S.TA MARIA GALRES
CHANNEL OF S.TA ROSA
S.TA ROSA ISLAND
GULF OF MEXICO
British Miles
86 West Longitude

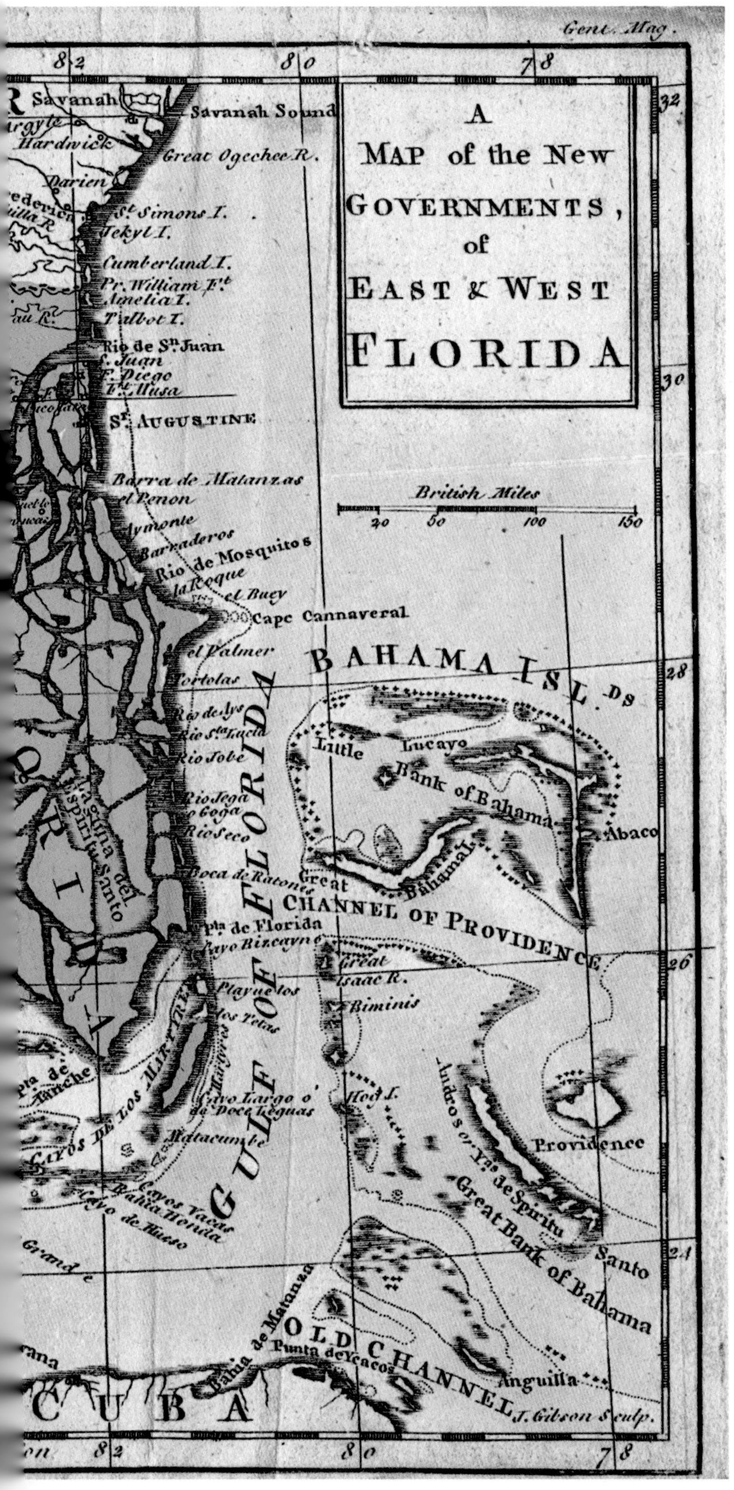

PLATE 4.2. *A Map of the New Government of East and West Florida*, 1763. Showing the boundary lines of British East and West Florida with an inset depicting Pensacola Bay. From *Gentleman's Magazine*, 33 (November 1763). Copy on file in John C. Pace Library, Special Collections, University of West Florida, Pensacola. Hand colored by Nancy Miller.

the transfers. In the fall of 1763, the British military reached Pensacola. One year later, civilian government arrived in the person of George Johnstone, a thirty-three-year-old Scot. Distinguished by both his bravery and his volatile temper, this first governor of the West Florida colony owed his position to political connections in England rather than to experience. And he had a tall order to fill, which included establishing civilian government, attracting settlers to the colony, maintaining good Indian relations, and establishing trade with the Spanish in Louisiana.[2]

Johnstone appointed a twelve-member Council, or upper house legislature, composed of influential citizens, which included the likes of Elias Durnford, surveyor general of West Florida; Sir John Lindsay, commander of British Naval forces in Pensacola; and James McPherson, secretary of the Province. Durnford was a surveyor, urban planner, and artist. His paintings of Havana—perhaps completed during the British occupation of the Cuban port city in 1762—are those of an accomplished artist. He surveyed large portions of West Florida and completely redesigned the town of Pensacola but apparently did not find time to paint a single scene. Sir John Lindsay was a British naval officer who arrived in Pensacola aboard the HMS *Tartar*. He and his ship were well known for their roles in a major navigational breakthrough—testing the efficacy of Nelson Harrison's timepiece in the measurement of longitude. A Pensacola street, Lindsay Street, was named after him and a navigational point at the entrance to Pensacola Bay, Tartar Point, was named for his ship. James McPherson was a writer as well as secretary of the council. Years after he departed Pensacola, McPherson became a member of the British Parliament and earned dubious renown for creating a fictitious ancient Scottish poet and fabricating his supposed works in *The Poems of Ossian*. The appointments of these men demonstrate the elite nature of the upper-house legislature in West Florida.[3]

Eligible white male voters in the colony elected a fourteen-member assembly, or lower house legislature. With strong support from this assembly, Johnstone introduced civilian government to West Florida. Of the forty-seven bills passed by this legislature during the British period, fifteen passed while he governed.[4]

Settlement

As for the town Johnstone inherited, the great majority of its buildings were small, wooden, and nondescript, lacking in such common amenities as chimneys and windows. The only substantial structure was the old Spanish governor's house. But the location of the town was good. Situated on the northern Gulf Coast and shielded by a barrier island and a peninsula that is today Gulf Breeze, Pensacola was strategically located for the purposes of trade and empire building and partially insulated from the tropical storms that blew through between June and December. Moreover, it was bounded by two freshwater streams that provided not only natural boundaries for the community but also excellent sources of potable water. Satisfied with the settlement site, if not the built environment, Johnstone set himself to establishing a proper British town on the shores of Pensacola Bay.

For this task, the governor turned to Elias Durnford, his surveyor general, who laid out a large grid on the landscape, one that paralleled the bay shore. At the heart of the town was the fort, which served the same purpose as it did in the Spanish era, projecting the power of an empire while defending a frontier coastal town. On each side of the fort was an open space and beyond that lots—twenty-eight blocks in all—fronted by streets named after British kings, war heroes, and politicians. Although a town lot could be obtained at no cost, it came with expenses: an annual quit rent (property tax) of six English pence, the requirement to build on it within two years and to fence it with a five-foot-high fence; the last requirement mirrored prevailing enclosure laws in the mother country. Almost every town lot had an accompanying garden lot to the north, at the site of modern-day Garden Street.[5]

Those with land titles purchased from the departing Spanish had the first choice of town lots. British military officers and bureaucrats came next. These first claimants—men like James Noble, Elias Durnford, John Lindsay, and James McPherson—chose waterfront lots on the western bay shore where breezes were stiff, fresh water plentiful, and defense seemingly secure (based on plans to build a military blockhouse in the area). These members of the elite upper class also acquired former Spanish plantations, or haciendas, in the bay interior. But as these estates were somewhat remote, the owners tended to live in their town houses.

In 1765, British Navy cartographer George Gauld depicted the new British town. A surveyor, naval cartographer, and artist, Gauld arrived in Pensacola in 1764 and later became a member of the American Philosophical Society, which promoted the exploration and mapping of North America. Meticulously mapping the coastline and inland waterways of the Gulf Coast, Gauld was a forerunner in the expanding cartography movement in North America. Along with his contemporaries—Dr. John Lorimer of Pensacola and William Bartram and Bernard Romans, noted chroniclers of West Florida who visited Pensacola—Gauld helped to lay the foundations for later explorations and mapping projects, including the Lewis and Clark Expedition.

In a painting entitled "A View of Pensacola," Gauld detailed both the architecture of the town and the ships in the harbor. The houses along the bay shore and inside the fort appear to be of Spanish origin with British modifications, such as the addition of chimneys and windows. The Spanish governor's house is the most substantial of the structures. Others are quite modest, with walls of wood or plaster and roofs of thatch or wooden shingles. All reflect a strong West Indian architecture rather than the more formal Georgian style prevailing in the more affluent and established Atlantic Seaboard colonies at the time. On the eastern edge of town is a cluster of houses labeled Indian

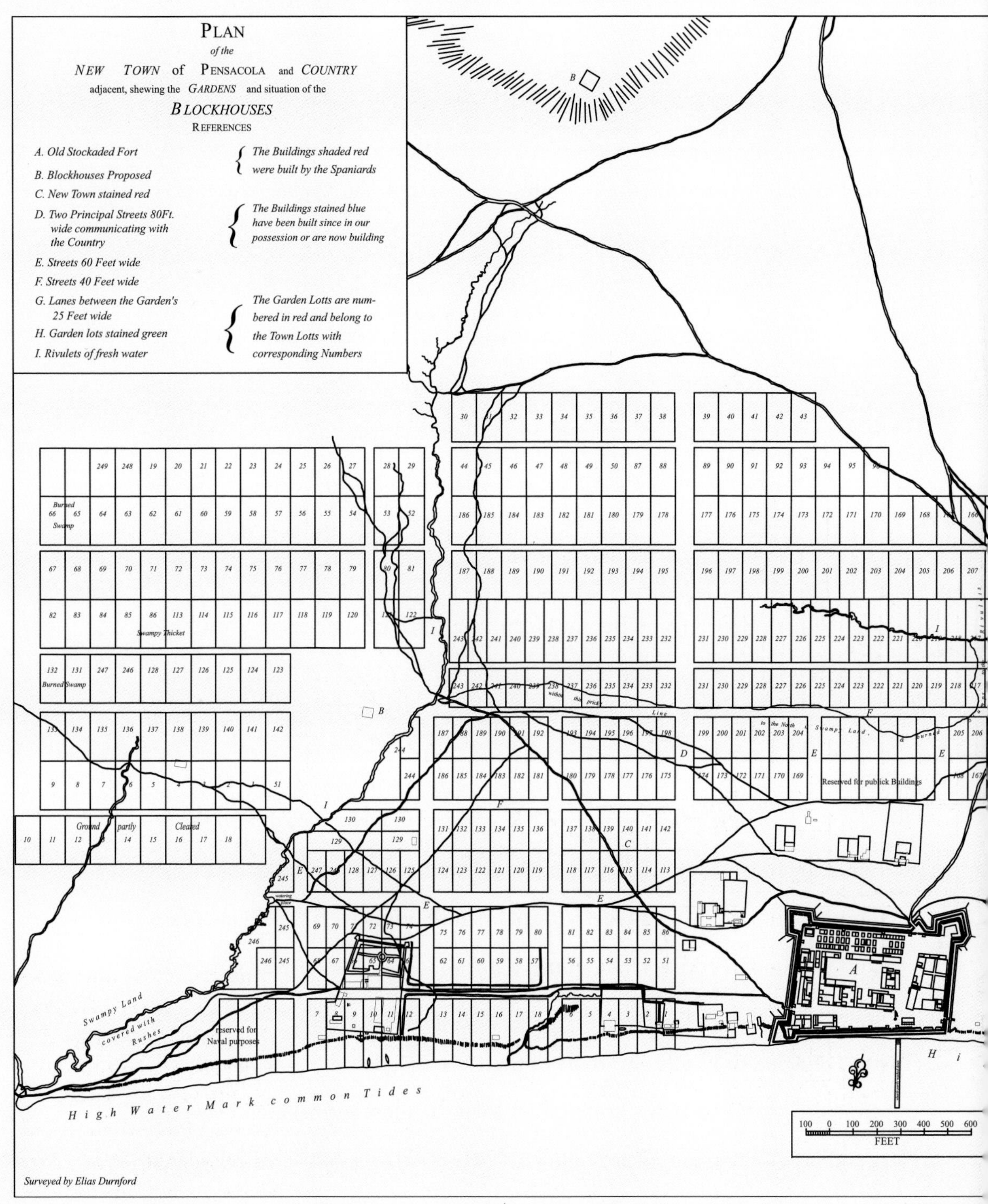
PLAN
of the
NEW TOWN of PENSACOLA and COUNTRY
adjacent, shewing the GARDENS and situation of the
BLOCKHOUSES
REFERENCES
A. Old Stockaded Fort
B. Blockhouses Proposed
C. New Town stained red
D. Two Principal Streets 80Ft. wide communicating with the Country
E. Streets 60 Feet wide
F. Streets 40 Feet wide
G. Lanes between the Garden's 25 Feet wide
H. Garden lots stained green
I. Rivulets of fresh water
The Buildings shaded red were built by the Spaniards
The Buildings stained blue have been built since in our possession or are now building
The Garden Lotts are numbered in red and belong to the Town Lotts with corresponding Numbers
Burned Swamp
Swampy Thicket
Burned Swamp
Ground partly Cleared
within this pricked Line
to the North Swamp Land, burned
Reserved for publick Buildings
Swampy Land covered with Rushes
reserved for Naval purposes
watering place
High Water Mark common Tides
100 0 100 200 300 400 500 600
FEET
Surveyed by Elias Durnford

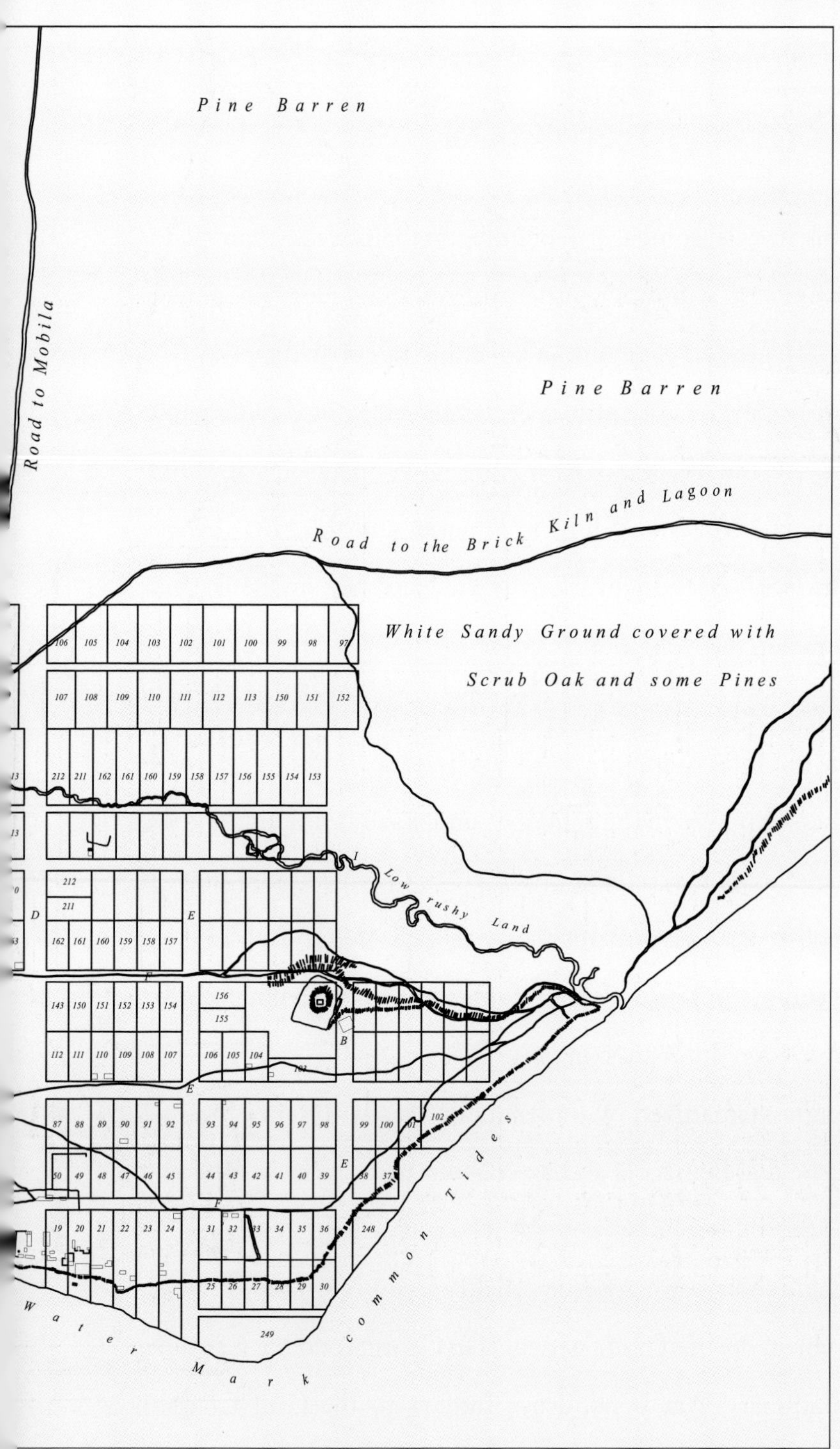

FIGURE 4.1. Composite drawing of Elias Durnford's town plan. Digitized and adapted from photographic reproduction PRO Co 700 No. 20 town and PRO MPG 528 fort. Courtesy of University of West Florida Archaeology Institute.

Town. A closer look reveals women with bundles on their heads—rare pictorial evidence of women in a frontier settlement—and a young boy playing with a dog. In the foreground are a number of ships and boats.

Archaeologist Coz Cozzi has identified the larger vessels in Gauld's painting as the HMS *Active*, the flagship of Rear Admiral William Burnaby, commander in chief of His Majesty's Ships at Jamaica, and the HMS *Alarm*, another ship in Burnaby's fleet. Identifiable by the flags they are flying, these ships were positioned in the foreground to obscure the open areas to the east and west of the fort, which are today Seville Square and Plaza Ferdinand. Smaller vessels in the foreground are most likely John Lindsay's schooner, the *Tartar*, and the sloop *Ferret*. The schooner under sail is unidentified but may represent one of several private vessels used by George Gauld himself. This water perspective of the new British town is dedicated to Burnaby and likely executed to commemorate the admiral's visit to Pensacola for an Indian congress called by George Johnstone in 1765.

The Indian congress organized by Johnstone in 1765 was the first of two Indian congresses held at Pensacola and drew about 500 Creeks to the town. In 1771, Governor Peter Chester (1770–1781), who succeeded Johnstone after a series of interim and short-term governors, held a second congress. These efforts, along with a breakdown of trade networks in Georgia and the Carolinas during the Revolutionary War years, drove Indians to the Gulf Coast in search of the European goods that they had become so dependent upon.

Facilitating Indian relations in British West Florida was Alexander

PLATE 4.3 Architectural styles of structures along the shoreline and people as depicted in *A View of Pensacola in West Florida* by George Gauld, ca. 1765. Library of Congress. Hand colored by Dave Edwards. Courtesy of University of West Florida Archaeology Institute.

McGillivray, an Indian commissary to the Creeks. Born to a Scottish father and a French/Creek mother, McGillivray maintained close ties to his mother's people. When American patriots confiscated his father's landholdings, McGillivray became an avowed enemy of the American cause and an integral part of Britain's Indian policy.[6] Despite the efforts of men like McGillivray, Johnstone, and Chester, the British proved little more capable than the Spanish had been in attracting a large resident Indian population to live in and around the town. In an effort to attract European settlers, the British engaged in a number of recruitment schemes.

In 1765–1766, Montfort Browne, Johnstone's lieutenant governor, oversaw the immigration of four-dozen Huguenots to Pensacola to cultivate silkworms and grapes. Arriving in January 1766, the French Calvinists settled Campbell Town, a small community on the bay, about ten miles east of Pensacola. Although Elias Durnford platted the lots of the new town, little is known about the spatial layout of the community. However, along with houses for the colonists there was a cemetery that served both Campbell Town and Pensacola. For several years the immigrants of Campbell Town struggled to survive in the sandy soils of Northwest Florida while battling recurrences of epidemic disease. Factors such as these no doubt made the cemetery an active component of the community. Although Pensacola continued to grow, Campbell Town foundered and was abandoned within six years. Contemporary with the Huguenot migration, Montfort Browne apparently brought 200 Irish indentured servants to the colony to work on his family's

PLATE 4.4. Indians trading deerskins for British goods in Pensacola. Painting by Dave Edwards. Courtesy of University of West Florida Archaeology Institute.

land grant on Dauphin Island, the barrier island to the west of Pensacola. The island proved unsuitable to large-scale agriculture, and the family's title to the property came into dispute. Soon thereafter the lieutenant governor abandoned the Irish, who were left to their own devices.[7]

One group of immigrants came not as religious dissenters or indentured servants but as chattel slaves. In the Atlantic Seaboard colonies and in the western portions of the West Florida colony, slaves labored on plantations. In the pineywoods around Pensacola, however, they worked in water-powered sawmill complexes, on the wharves, and in the houses of government bureaucrats and military officers. Arriving primarily via Jamaica, these industrial and house slaves were little more than numbers during their lifetimes and are largely lost to history. One exception is Maria Belle, a slave acquired by Sir John Lindsay several years prior to his posting in Pensacola and who apparently accompanied him to Pensacola in 1764. When Lindsay left Pensacola for England in 1765, Belle apparently was with him. Nothing is known of her life in Pensacola from 1764 to 1765. However, when Lindsay left Pensacola for England in 1765, Belle went with him. While her life in England was lived in the shadows, she probably enjoyed a relatively sheltered and comfortable life protected and provided for by Lindsay. What is known is that their relationship produced a daughter, Dido Elizabeth Belle, who from early childhood lived with Lindsay's uncle, Lord Mansfield (who is credited with effectively freeing the slaves in England by his decision in the famous Somerset Case).

In January of 1774, Lindsay deeded the lot he still owned in the Pensacola navy yard to Maria Belle, described as a "Negro Woman of Pensacola in

PLATE 4.5. A Portrait of Admiral John Lindsay by James Tassie, ca. 1795. Courtesy of Mallett PLC, London, 2006.

FIGURE 4.2. Artist's interpretation of Maria Belle in silhouette. Courtesy of Nancy Miller and model Alesia Ross, University of West Florida Archaeology Institute.

PLATE 4.6. Dido Elizabeth Belle Lindsay and her cousin Lady Elizabeth Murray. Johann Zoffany, *Elizabeth Murray and Dido Belle*, ca. 1780. By kind permission from the collection of the Earl of Mansfield, Scone Palace, Scotland.

America but now of London afore and made free." There are bits of evidence to suggest that Maria Belle did return to Pensacola, leaving behind John Lindsay, who had taken a wife, and her daughter, Dido. Seven months after Lindsay deeded Belle a town lot, a woman named Maria Belle paid a manumission price of $200 to one Phillips Comyn in Pensacola, perhaps to cement her freedom in British West Florida. Lindsay stipulated that Belle build a house and fence in the lot. A 1778 map of Pensacola seems to confirm that she did both, as it shows a new house standing on an enclosed lot.

Artifacts recovered from a well and storage pit believed to be associated with the house reflect a comfortable life with access to a wide range of British wares. Archaeologists found watermelon seeds, peanut hulls, beans, peach pits, domestic and nondomestic animal bones, and fish bones in the well. A Spanish olive jar with cordage attached to the neck rested at the bottom of the well, suggesting that the vessel was being used as a bucket for drawing water or as a counter weight. The olive jar may be evidence of illegal trade with the Spanish or simply an example of early recycling—since the military received olive oil as part of the ordinance provisions for the fort. However, the presence of such a prominent Spanish cultural marker at the bottom of a British-era well on property owned by an ex-slave is suggestive of the melding of cultures in the multiracial, multi-ethnic Caribbean Basin.[8]

Many settlers came not as religious dissenters, indentured servants, or slaves but as small planters and farmers looking for cheap land or political asylum. Although not all of the land in the colony was suitable for farming,

PLATE 4.7. Table setting illustrating artifacts recovered from Lot Six (including wine glass stems, glass decanter stopper, creamware, white salt-glazed stoneware, and Nottingham mug sherds). Photograph by Al Audleman. Courtesy of University of West Florida Archaeology Institute.

it was cheap and in many cases free. And West Florida was loyalist territory during the Revolutionary War years. Settlers descended on Pensacola from the Atlantic Seaboard colonies, arriving via the Ohio and Mississippi river systems, sailing around the Florida peninsula, or trekking overland through Georgia. Some Frenchmen from Louisiana migrated to British West Florida rather than live under Spanish rule, and German soldiers filled out the ranks of the military in Pensacola during the American Revolution.

PLATE 4.8. Bottom barrel of an excavated barrel-lined well feature that was later used as a trash pit. (Note: The barrel was in a good state of preservation because it was submerged in the airtight environment below the water table. A well point de-watering system was utilized to lower the water table within the excavation unit approximately 3' to allow for recovery of the barrel and its contents.) An intact olive jar with cordage attached to the neck was resting at the bottom of the well suggesting that it was being used as a "bucket." Both the well and an adjacent excavated barrel-lined storage pit are associated with the house on Lot Six ca. 1778. Courtesy of University of West Florida Archaeology Institute.

These foreigners might have included French Huguenots and German Lutherans. Most English settlers were of the Anglican tradition. This tradition, however, did not result in the construction of a formal church. Anglican religious services took place in private homes, much like other social and cultural activities. Settlers gathered in private homes or in one of the numerous taverns around town to drink tea, ale, or punch and to discuss the day's events. Unfortunately, the day's events too often revolved around sickness and death.

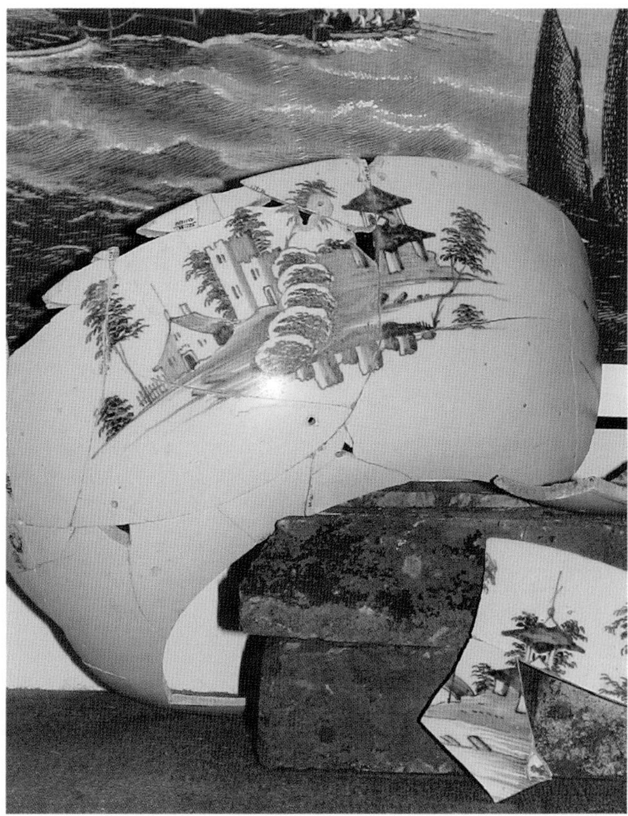

PLATE 4.9. Delft punchbowl, one of several punchbowls recovered from the area of the Commanding Officers' Compound of the Fort of Pensacola. Courtesy of University of West Florida Archaeology Institute.

Survival: Until Sickness and Death Do Us Part

Sickness and death were constant companions of the soldiers and settlers at Pensacola. In all, about one-fifth of the town's residents perished between 1765 and 1767, due primarily to yellow fever. Among the dead was one of the most important military figures in America's early history, General Henry Bouquet. Having received acclaim for his heroics on behalf of the British colonists in the French and Indian War, Bouquet came to Pensacola in the summer of 1765 as a newly appointed brigadier general. As his ship set anchor in the bay, the town was in the midst of a virulent outbreak of yellow fever, with a death rate hovering around ten to twelve a day. Bouquet himself quickly fell victim to the mosquito-borne disease. He developed chills and fever. The whites of his eyes and his skin yellowed. His liver and kidneys failed, and he succumbed to yellow fever in September 1765.

Dr. John Lorimer spearheaded efforts to improve health conditions at Pensacola and combat the sort of epidemic that took Bouquet's life. Under the Spanish, Fort San Miguel had been a completely enclosed stockade, with its south side walled off from the sea breezes blowing off the bay. The fact that Spanish structures inside the fort lacked windows created a stifling situation for soldiers dressed in wool uniforms. The lack of ventilation also incubated mosquitoes. In the renovation of the old Spanish fort, the British removed the south side stockade wall to allow for sea breezes and facilitate the circulation of fresh air. They also added windows to previously windowless structures. Lorimer recommended draining the swamps around the town, constructing privies, and boiling drinking water—indicating that he was ahead of his time in trying to stem the transmission of diseases. The degree to which his recommendations were carried out is unclear, as recurring epidemics of yellow fever, dysentery, typhus, typhoid fever, and malaria made life on the bay a precarious endeavor. Many settlers ended their days in Pensacola in the cemetery located on the northern outskirts of the community.[9]

Others suffered from scurvy, which ravages a body depleted of vitamin C. To combat scurvy, soldiers planted fruit trees and vegetable gardens inside and outside the fort. Fruits like peaches and watermelons thrived in the sandy environment, but most fruits and vegetables did not. There were, however, pockets of good soil around town. In 1770, Robert Carkett, captain of the HMS *Lowestoft*, commandeered a lot adjacent to John Lindsay's in the navy yard where he raised vegetables and chickens to supply the king's ships; Carkett noted that the seeds and plants "throve surprisingly well" in the soil—not surprising as they were rooted in the rich midden deposits (decomposing shells and organic material) left by the native peoples who occupied the site prior to European arrival. The fresh vegetables no doubt warded off a good many cases of scurvy. In general, the basic nutritional needs of the majority of the soldiers and settlers in British Pensacola were being met, and the community was supplied with salted and pickled beef, pork, rice, peas, fruit, and rum.

Every man, woman, and child—from Indian to tradesman and craftsman, from military officer to planter, from intellectual to slave—relied on a maritime economy that exported furs and naval stores and imported staple goods and luxury items. Despite the fact that the Spanish had failed to wrest a profit from Pensacola and West Florida, eighteenth-century British approached the venture with an in-bred sense of superiority. Major Augustin Prevost, the first military commander of the town, suggested that Spanish laziness rather than the infertility of the land afflicted Pensacola: "The country from the insuperable laziness of the Spaniards remains still uncultivated, the woods are close to the village and a few paltry gardens show the only improvements. The climate is not healthy, the soil around the village though sandy is able to produce vegetables; further back the country is good and capable of improvement—but years and a number of industrious settlers can only make a change upon the face of the colony." Prevost reflected long-held attitudes regarding Spanish industriousness or lack thereof, part of the so-called Black Legend dating back to at least the sixteenth century. He also exemplified an entrenched belief in British ethnic superiority.[10]

However, many British officials and resident merchants saw great promise in the Spanish trade, given the proximity of Pensacola to New Orleans, Havana, Veracruz, and other Spanish ports. Such trade was legal for British subjects under only one condition: if goods were carried on British ships in accordance with the Navigation Acts, the century-old laws designed to regulate commerce and undercut Dutch competition. The Acts that laid the seeds of the American Revolution prevented Spanish ships from calling on

Pensacola. Initially, British military officers enforced the regulation and barred Spanish ships from entering the port. Major William Forbes, the second military commander at Pensacola, regularly seized Spanish ships at Pensacola, all the while urging the government to allow such trade. The first civilian governor George Johnstone continuously called for a slackening of the mercantilist laws but got no cooperation from officials in London. With no compromise in sight, merchants who had relocated their businesses to Pensacola with the intent of tapping into the Spanish trade began to abandon the colony. It appeared that the future of West Florida was at stake unless sound reasoning prevailed on the issue.

Sound reasoning did not prevail in the end—neither under Johnstone nor any of his successors, but the Spanish trade occurred nonetheless. In the late 1760s, several Spanish ships called at Pensacola, and British merchants even took up residence in Spanish New Orleans. As before, the fluid frontier environment won out over impractical, mercantilist policy. But the 1770s brought more restrictions on trade. Bernard Romans, who toured West Florida in the mid-1770s and wrote *A Concise and Natural History of East and West Florida*, reported that the ban on the Spanish trade "has led many to ruin."

British merchants did foster the Indian fur trade in the West Florida colony, but those resident in Pensacola depended heavily on the naval stores industries—pitch, tar, and turpentine used in ship construction—and in the production of staves and shingles; archaeologist John Phillips finds evidence of these industries in the remains of the water-powered mills that once dotted the landscape of Northwest Florida. Pensacola, isolated physically and economically from the more fertile western portions of the West Florida colony and from the long-established economic centers of the eastern seaboard, was somewhat removed from events unfolding in the course of the American Revolution.[11]

Twilight of the British Era

In the decade and a half between 1763 and 1778, Pensacola evolved from a frontier Spanish outpost into a settled British town. The fort itself was expanded and redesigned several times. John Muller's *A Treatise Containing the Elementary Part of Fortification*, published in 1746, proposed that fortified places by the sea or on other bodies of water function mainly to protect and promote trade. Muller's *Treatise* may have greatly influenced the Pensacola fortification as West Florida was primarily a commercial venture. However, despite treatises and the best intentions of military engineers, the effects of semi-tropical moisture, coupled with the occasional hurricane, created an ongoing cycle of construction and repair in British Pensacola. A 1778 hurricane best illustrates the effects of catastrophic forces on the town.

The October 9, 1778, log of the HMS *Sylph* recorded a powerful hurricane that ran aground all of the vessels in the bay and destroyed many structures on shore with high winds and storm surges of eleven or twelve feet. Witnessing the damage done to the fleet, fort, and structures around town

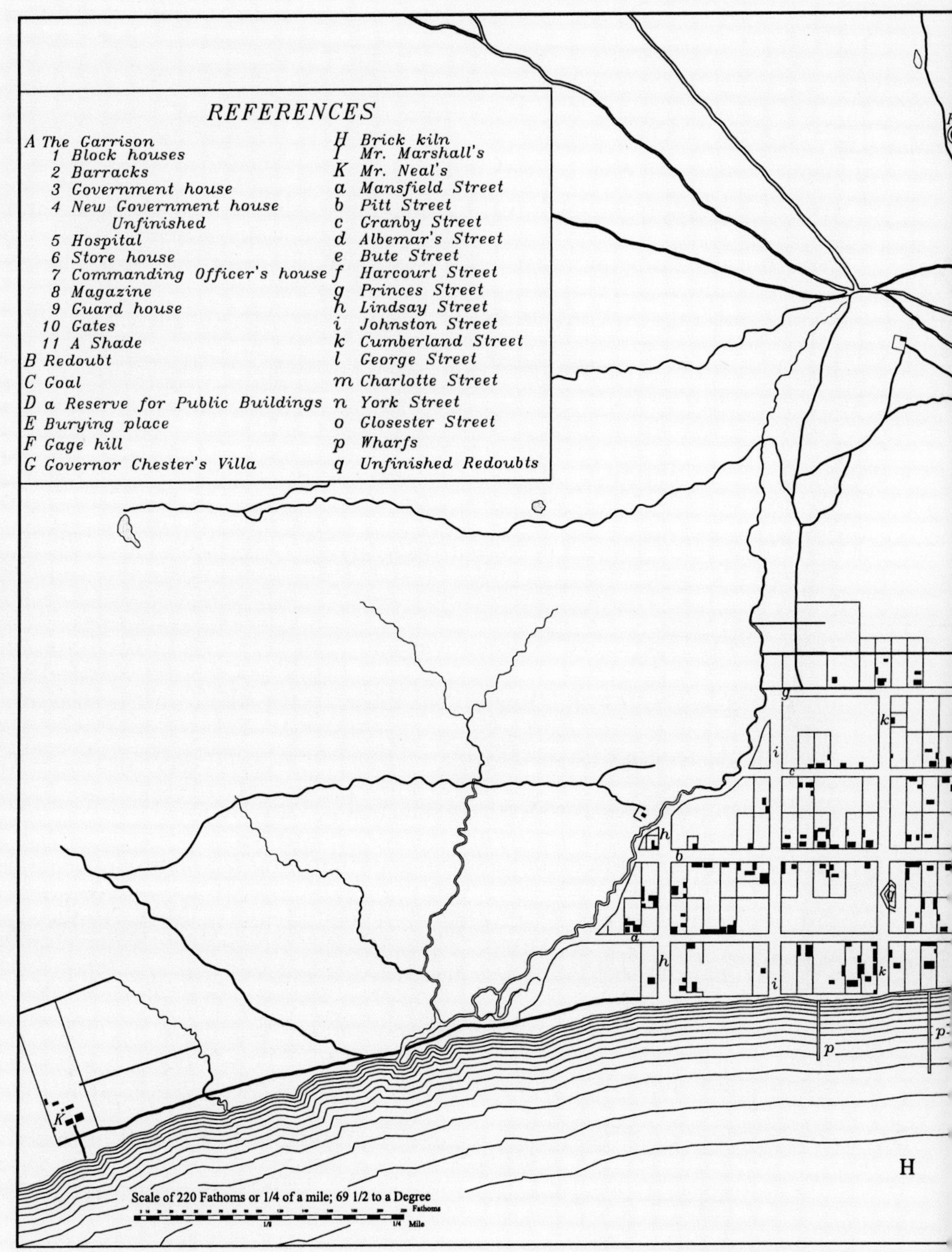
REFERENCES
A The Garrison
1 Block houses
2 Barracks
3 Government house
4 New Government house Unfinished
5 Hospital
6 Store house
7 Commanding Officer's house
8 Magazine
9 Guard house
10 Gates
11 A Shade
B Redoubt
C Goal
D a Reserve for Public Buildings
E Burying place
F Gage hill
G Governor Chester's Villa
H Brick kiln
I Mr. Marshall's
K Mr. Neal's
a Mansfield Street
b Pitt Street
c Granby Street
d Albemar's Street
e Bute Street
f Harcourt Street
g Princes Street
h Lindsay Street
i Johnston Street
k Cumberland Street
l George Street
m Charlotte Street
n York Street
o Glosester Street
p Wharfs
q Unfinished Redoubts
H
Scale of 220 Fathoms or 1/4 of a mile; 69 1/2 to a Degree
Fathoms
1/8
1/4
Mile

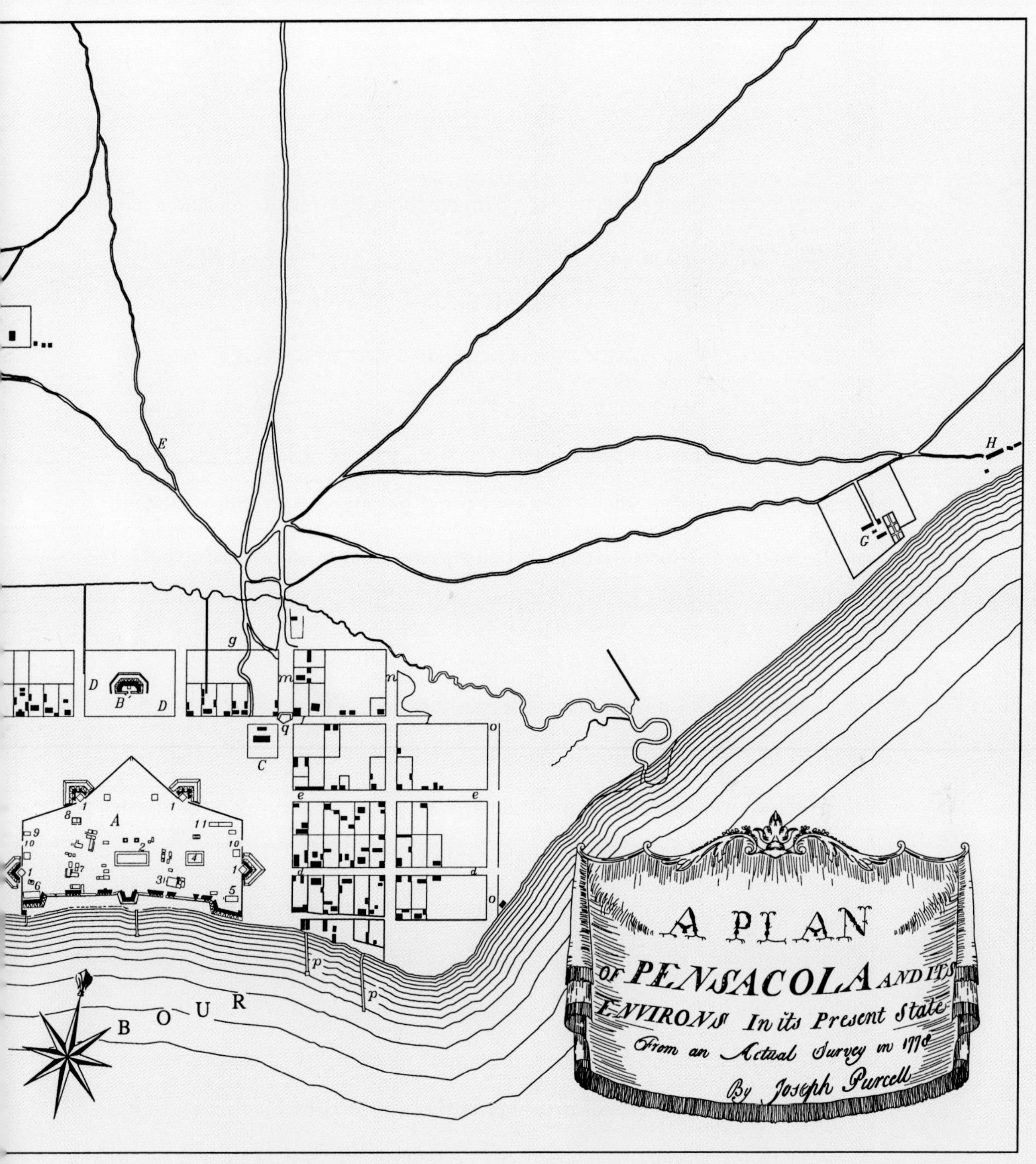

FIGURE 4.3. *A Plan of Pensacola and its environs*. . . by Joseph Purcell, 1778. Digitized and adapted. Library of Congress, Geography and Map Division. Courtesy of University of West Florida Archaeology Institute.

Governor Peter Chester declared the damage the worst in a decade and a half of British rule. In the storm's aftermath, soldiers and settlers set themselves to repairing the town, unaware that within a few years it, along with the rest of the colony of West Florida, would be reigned over by a foreign king.

During the early stages of the war, Pensacola and West Florida remained outside the mainstream of conflict in the American Revolution. There were many reasons that the colony and its capital remained peaceful, and loyal, during the war. Historian Robin Fabel suggests that vocal and disgruntled lower house legislators were more interested in unseating unpopular governor Peter Chester than in rejecting the authority of King George III. Moreover, there had always been a strong military presence in Pensacola that acted as a deterrent to rebellion. Finally, there was an apathetic population that paid little in the way of taxes and had little patience for the destruction that came with a revolution. They wanted to make money, not war.

Also, colonists in West Florida did not feel the effects of the Stamp Act or the Townshend Revenue Act, legislation that pushed British colonists to rebellion elsewhere. And their experience with rebellions was not positive. In 1778, James Willing, a former resident of Natchez, had descended the Mississippi to stir up a rebellion in the southernmost British colonies. In the course of trying to stir loyal subjects to rebellion, he destroyed and seized property of colonists in West Florida.

Unwilling to rebel in support of the American cause, the British colonists soon found themselves under a Spanish flag due to the exploits of an illustrious young Louisiana governor named Bernardo de Gálvez, who had the benefit of emerging on the scene at a crucial time in the Atlantic World. During the American Revolution, Gálvez assumed a leading role on a very visible stage. Coming to the Louisiana governorship in 1777, his timing was good. Spain, though reluctant to aid a group of rebels who were setting such a bad example for its own colonists to the south, allied itself with France against England in a secret treaty signed in April 1779.

When news of the alliance reached New Orleans, Bernardo de Gálvez sprang into action. Having already banned trade with the British, he seized British vessels on the Mississippi and expelled British merchants from New Orleans. Subsequently, he turned his attention to expelling British troops from West Florida. Beginning in September 1779, he drove them from the lower Mississippi River, first at Manchac then at Baton Rouge. He then set his sights on Mobile and Pensacola. As the head of more than 1,300 troops, Gálvez captured Mobile in March 1780. A year later he anchored a large force off Santa Rosa Island. After two months of bloody battles that resulted in almost 300 British and Spanish casualties, Gálvez captured Pensacola on May 8, 1781. Unlike the impoverished frontier settlement that the Spanish had abandoned almost two decades before, the one they inherited from the British was a thriving port town with an established maritime economy.[12]

The Battle of Pensacola, as it came to be known, was important to the American cause in that Britain lost a valuable port by which it could have landed troops and supplies and protected its interests along the Gulf Coast.

Moreover, the victory gave the Americans leverage at the peace tables of Paris. And finally, the Spanish got their Florida possessions back. Bernardo de Galvéz, with a roll of the dice, had initiated a second era of Spanish rule in West Florida. For his heroic actions, in 2012, Galvez was designated a *Great Floridian* for his significant contributions to the progress and welfare of Florida. In 2014, the United States conferred honorary citizenship on Galvez in recognition of his contributions in our nation's struggle for independence.

Summary

Today, the site of the British town of Pensacola is incorporated in the Seville Historic District, a nine-block area in the heart of downtown. Within the confines of the city's historic district, businesses, private homes, art museums, bars, and restaurants abound. Along with the Colonial Archaeology Trail (that exposes foundation remains of the British fort along its meandering path), the T. T. Wentworth Museum of Florida History, the Pensacola Historical Society Museum, and the Archaeology Institute on the University of West Florida campus offer the reader opportunities to learn what life was like in British Pensacola. However, the most enduring legacy of Pensacola's British past is not in the town's museums or archives but in the town itself. Modern Pensacola is a testament to the foresight of the gifted urban planner Elias Durnford. Residents would do well to raise a glass of Colonial Punch in his honor.

RECIPE: Colonial Punch

Punch is a popular drink around the world, and it was one of the most popular drinks in British colonial America. First tasted by colonial troops in India, it contained five ingredients: tea, arrack, sugar, lemons, and water. Americans added rum to the punch. Individuals, inns, and taverns took great pride in their recipes and jealously guarded them.

4 cups strong green tea
1 ½ pounds white sugar
1 cup hot water
6 lemons: juice and rind
1 quart rum

Pare the yellow rind of the lemons very thin; squeeze out and strain the juice. Stir rind, juice, and water into the tea; add the sugar and stir until it is all dissolved. Slowly pour in one quart of good rum and stir again. Cool and serve in cups or glasses over a little shaved ice—background and recipe by Catherine Parker.

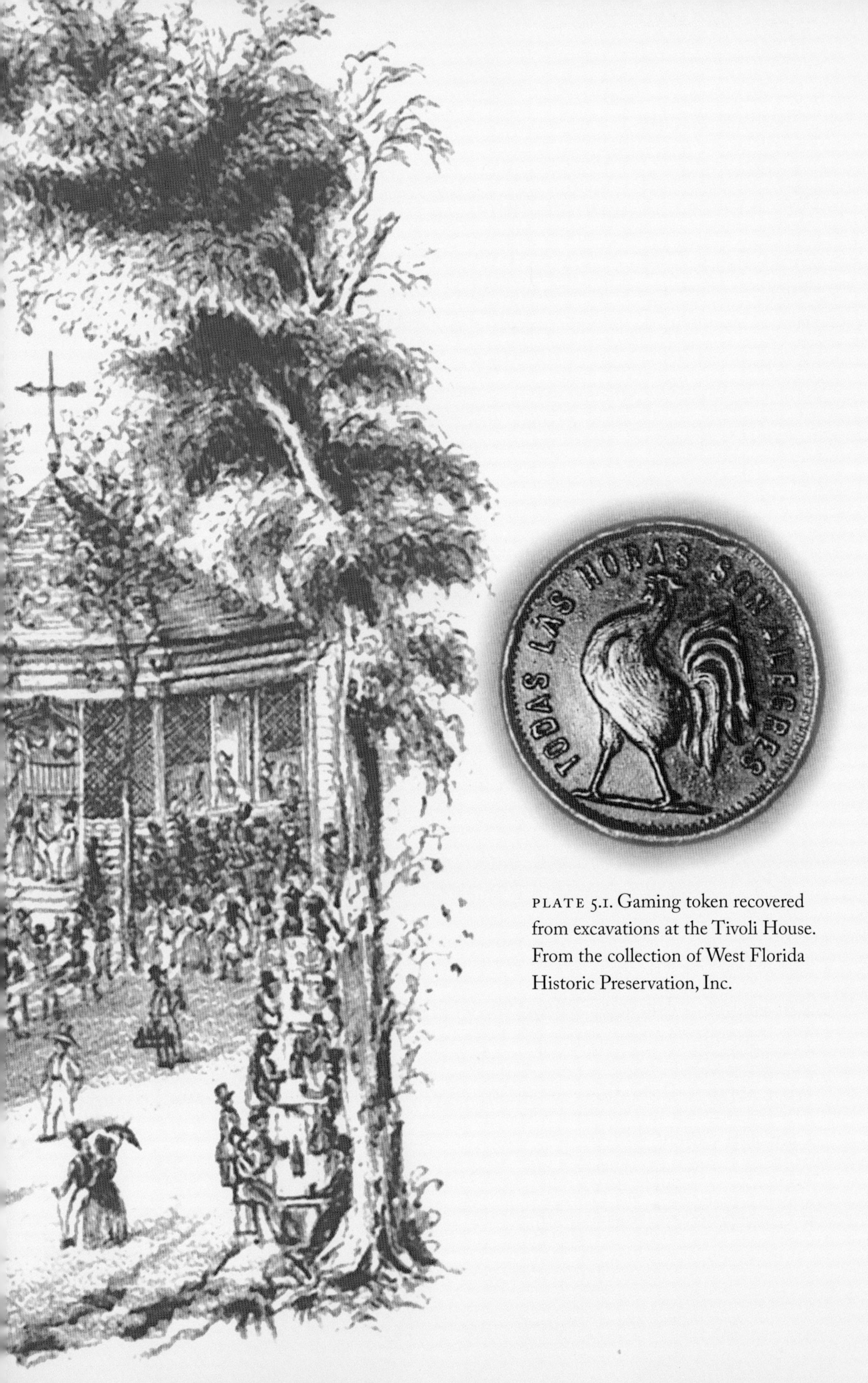

PLATE 5.1. Gaming token recovered from excavations at the Tivoli House. From the collection of West Florida Historic Preservation, Inc.

FIVE

Second Spanish Period
1781–1821

Dancing was universally popular as were card parties and devotees made no distinction as to the day of the week on which they pursued their pleasure.

—Historian Lyle McAlister, "Pensacola during the Second Spanish Period"

A FRENCH ROOSTER ADORNS A SMALL COPPER TOKEN recovered by archaeologists at the site of the Tivoli House, a ballroom and entertainment venue that was at the physical and metaphorical heart of Pensacola during the "Second Spanish Period." Perhaps used as a gaming piece at one of the Tivoli's card tables, the token is a reminder of the establishment's colorful past and a link to the diverse clientele who gathered there for dancing, dining, and gambling at the turn of the nineteenth century.

The history of the Pensacola Tivoli begins in 1804 when three Frenchmen from New Orleans, John B. Cazenave, Pedro Bardinave, and Rene Chardiveneau, purchased adjoining lots in the center of the Gulf Coast port town for the purpose of establishing a public house described as a *sala para la sanidad* or, loosely translated, a "recreation room." A year later, the three began construction on a ballroom and entertainment complex modeled after the New Orleans Tivoli. They adapted to Pensacola the Tivoli-style entertainment and inclusiveness, which they had experienced firsthand in New

PLATE 5.2 a and b. Watercolor of the Tivoli House. Courtesy of David Dodson. And a drawing (*on facing page*) of the New Orleans Tivoli as depicted on the cover of sheet music, *Valse de Tivoli*, Rosella Roussel par H. Rolling. Courtesy of Historic New Orleans Collection.

Orleans. Just as the Crescent City venue was open to all strata of society, so too was its Gulf Coast counterpart. In that sense, it stood as a testament to the diversity and intermingling of ethnicities along the coast. A gathering place for all, the Pensacola Tivoli was described as "a small, neat rotunda for public balls and adjacent public rooms for gaming." The original Pensacola Tivoli was just off an overgrown open space that is today picturesque Plaza Ferdinand, the urban park that commemorates the reign of Spanish King Ferdinand VII.

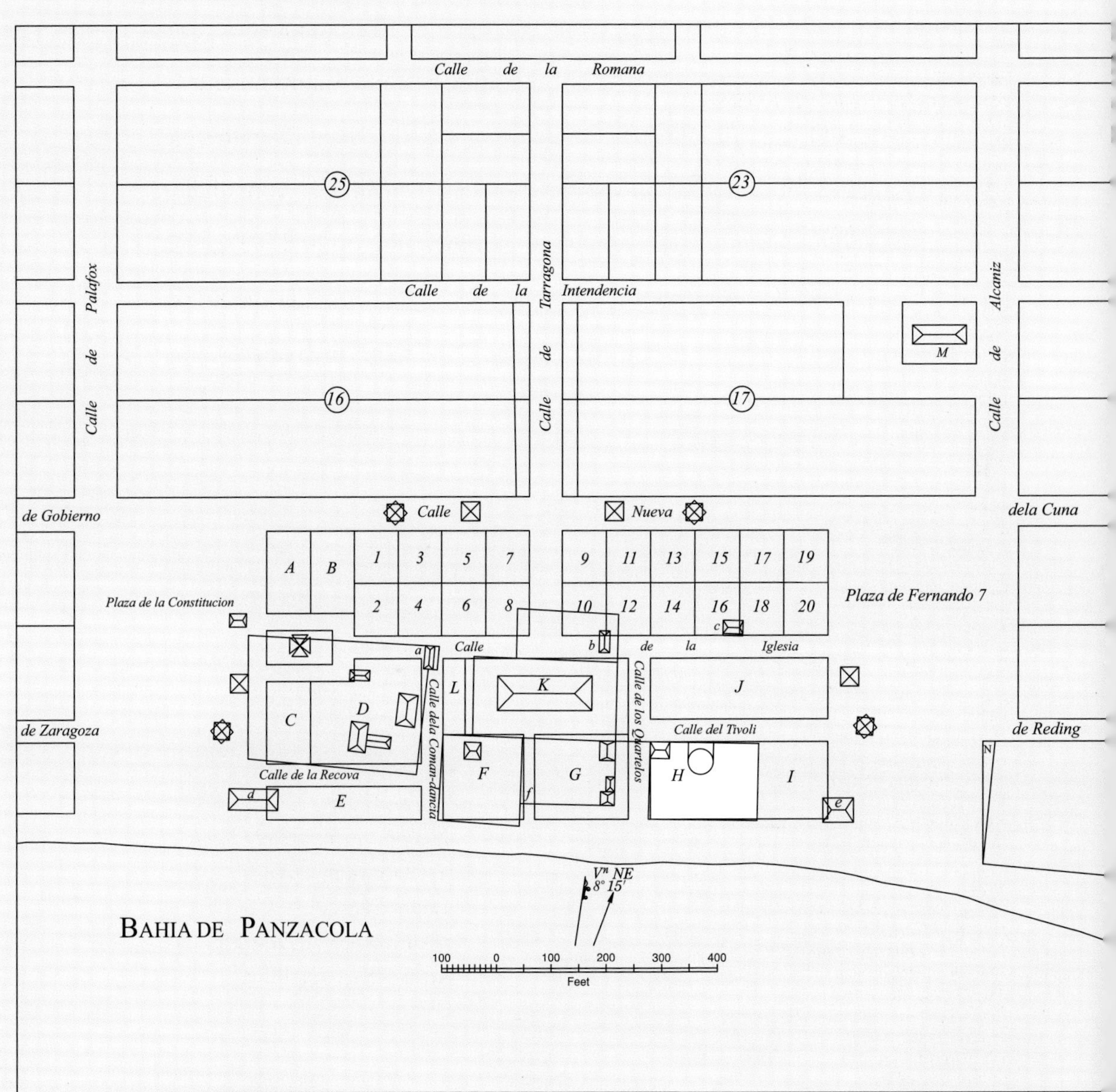
Calle de la Romana
Calle de la Intendencia
Calle de Palafox
Calle de Tarragona
Calle de Alcaniz
de Gobierno
Calle Nueva
dela Cuna
Plaza de la Constitucion
Plaza de Fernando 7
Calle de la Iglesia
Calle dela Coman-dancia
Calle de los Quartelos
Calle del Tivoli
de Zaragoza
de Reding
Calle de la Recova
25
23
16
17
M
A
B
C
D
E
F
G
H
I
J
K
L
a
b
c
d
e
f
N
1
2
3
4
5
6
7
8
9
10
11
12
13
14
15
16
17
18
19
20
Vn NE
8° 15′
BAHIA DE PANZACOLA
100 0 100 200 300 400
Feet

PLANO*

a) The Guard-house in ruins and the block-houses and other old buildings which remain in the squares and in the new street, which now serve for magazines and barracks will hereafter have to be demolished
b) The house in ruins
c) The present military kitchen
d) The present Church
e) The house in ruins
Lots suggested for following purposes:
☒) *for the Church*
A) for the consistory and principal Corps de Guard
B) for the Public jail
C) for the custom-house and revenue offices
D) reduced area on which the government houses stand and the garden
E) reserved for the market-house and public magazines
F) ground and house belonging to the Rev. James Coleman
G) houses and lot belonging to Grandpera and Tillas who relinquish 20 ft. lane (f)
H) lot on which stands the ball room and buildings of Cazenavo and Francisqui
I) ground reserved for a national hospital
J) grounds of old barracks which were burnt, reserved for eventual rebuilding and new kitchens
K) actual barracks with their yard to which two portions, E&W added and N&S taken off
L) lot for the building of the national magazines
M) the present public prison and principal Corps de Guard
1) lot for a public school
2) lot for parish vicar
3 to 20) salable lots
Reference: American State Papers, Public Lands, Vol IV
V.S. Pintado map for subdivision and public sale of lots
Black for planned, Red for actual lots and fences
dated Dec. 1, 1813
Signed by Pintado and Gomez

* Translation by Dr. W.S. Coker.

FIGURE 5.1. Pintado map of the Fort Grounds 1813 showing the location of the Tivoli House. Digitized from reproduction of Library of Congress MSS Div. Item 47, with legend translation. Courtesy of University of West Florida Archaeology Institute.

PLATE 5.3. Table setting illustrating tableware recovered from a well associated with the Tivoli House (coarse earthenwares, olive jar, faience, stoneware, wine bottle glass, peach pits). Photograph by Al Audleman. Courtesy of University of West Florida Archaeology Institute.

Perhaps appropriately, modern-day Plaza Ferdinand contains not a bust of Ferdinand VII but one of Andrew Jackson. Ferdinand was the vanquished Spanish king, the one who cowered in the wake of the Napoleonic invasion of Iberia, reigned over the dismantlement of a 300-year-old empire, and ceded the Floridas to the Americans. By contrast, Jackson is the victorious American general who won the Battle of New Orleans, the rough-hewn frontiersman who became the first territorial governor of Florida, and the American statesman who accepted the Floridas on behalf of the United States in a ceremony staged just off Plaza Ferdinand. Ferdinand's failures and Jackson's triumphs are indicative of Spanish misfortunes and American fortunes in the second Spanish period. In the decades following the forfeiture of Pensacola to the Americans, the United States came to be recognized as an emerging power in the Atlantic World. In 1781, with the nascent republic recovering from more than a half-decade of war, no one could have predicted such a scenario.

That year, the much acclaimed Charles III sat on the Spanish throne. Two decades into his reign, he had managed to right the Spanish ship through a broad ranging program of reform and rejuvenation. The Atlantic empires of Spain, England, and France were in flux. Spain's empire seemed destined to return to its former glory. Britain's, by contrast, appeared rudderless and adrift. The loss of the fifteen American colonies—East and West Florida plus the original thirteen—and the enormous debt acquired in the process had many British questioning the course of their empire. France's empire was in even worse shape. A corrupt government and a deteriorating national economy undermined the monarchy of the ill-fated Louis XVI. In the course of the American Revolution, Louis got his vengeance on the British for losses suffered in the French and Indian War, but French revolutionaries subsequently took vengeance on their king. Louis's death by guillotine in 1793 precipitated the empire of Napoleon Bonaparte, the abdication of Ferdinand VII, the demise of Spain's American empire, and, in an indirect way, the end of the Second Spanish Period in Pensacola.

Settlers

The population of Pensacola remained relatively small during the Second Spanish Period, despite efforts to entice settlers with offers of cheap land, no taxes, and religious toleration. The threat of Indian attack was no longer the deterrent that it once was. Nor were hurricanes, at least not according to the extant historical documents from the period. The threat of disease persisted, with deadly outbreaks of yellow fever in 1810 and 1811. But the number one deterrent remained the infertility of the soils in and around Pensacola. As in the British period, those migrating to West Florida preferred the fertile lands to the west rather than the sterile soils around Pensacola Bay.

In 1784, a diverse civilian population of about 300 lived in the town of Pensacola, while 800 Spanish soldiers bunked at Fort San Carlos de Barrancas, the reconstituted military stronghold on the bluffs overlooking the entrance to Pensacola Bay. Subsequent censuses in 1791 and 1802 reveal a civilian population of about 600, although these numbers likely do not take into account black slaves living in the area; some estimates have the slave population in the West Florida colony as a whole approaching or surpassing the white population. In 1805, on the heels of the Louisiana Purchase and the migration of French and Spanish residents of New Orleans to Pensacola, the civilian population of the town approximated 1,400. By the 1820 census the population was half that number, but it was as diverse as ever.[1]

Rachel Jackson, wife of Andrew, confirmed the kaleidoscope nature of the Pensacola population in a letter to friend Eliza Kingsley in 1821: "The inhabitants all speak Spanish and French. Some speak four or five languages. Such a mixed multitude, you, nor any of us, ever had an idea of. There are fewer white people by far than any other, mixed with all nations under the canopy of heaven, almost in nature's darkness."[2] Rachel Jackson looked upon the multi-ethnic, multiracial society with dismay, disdain, and prejudice; but this mixing pot of humanity on the shores of Pensacola Bay was one of the most open and accepting societies in North America.

A neighborhood on the west side of Pensacola best exemplified the town's unwritten policy of openness and toleration. Its residents included a Spanish port captain and his wife, a Canary Islander; a mulatto civil servant; a Spanish grocer and tavern owner, and his black common-law wife; an English carpenter; a free black laundress; Julee Panton, a free woman of color; Vincente Crespo, a Spanish butcher; Salvador Ruby, a prosperous mulatto shoemaker who owned several properties around town; and William Panton, a principal in Panton, Leslie and Company, a major commercial concern with a government-sanctioned monopoly on the Indian trade. Despite a lack of segregation in its neighborhoods, Pensacola was not without a clear social hierarchy, and ensconced at the top was the commandant.[3]

From 1781 to 1803, the commandant in Pensacola answered to a governor general in New Orleans and to a captain general in Havana. After the Louisiana Purchase, Pensacola became the seat of government in West Florida, and the commandant officially took on the title of governor. The longest serving and most prominent commandants/governors were Irishman Arturo O'Neill (1781–1793) and Catalonian Vicente Folch (1796–1810).[4]

As governor, Arturo O'Neill reestablished Spanish authority in Pensacola and maintained good relations with the Indians in the region. Although he called an Indian congress in 1784, he relied mostly on Alexander McGillivray and the principals of Panton, Leslie and Company to be his eyes and ears among the Indians. After many years of service in Pensacola, O'Neill departed the Gulf Coast to assume the post of captain general of Yucatan. The Irishman later rose to a ministerial post in Madrid. In 1808, at the age seventy-two, he fought in the Peninsular War against Napoleon's invading army and died a hero in his adopted country in 1814.

Vicente Folch's career was not so glorious and his death far less heralded. He was considered courageous and proud but also stubborn and difficult. As governor, Folch ordered a re-survey of the town with the purpose of identifying abandoned lots that could be sold by the Crown to generate sorely needed income for local government. Although controversial, the survey restored a sense of order to the town. That said, historian Jack Holmes characterized Folch's administration as one of "accomplishment, frustration, tyranny and final disgrace." Folch's antagonistic frontier policies hardly endeared him to the Indians or the British colonists to the north. Indians thought him to be a "madman," and American frontiersmen thought no better of him. Finally, unlike O'Neill, Folch did not use his service in Pensacola as a springboard to higher office. Dogged by charges of mismanagement in Pensacola, his career spiraled downward, and Folch died an impoverished man in Havana in 1829.

The great military challenge for officials like Folch and O'Neill was not to defend Pensacola against Indians or foreign enemies but to rein in Spanish soldiers who bunked outside town at Fort San Carlos de Barrancas. Those stationed at the fort comprised a raucous element. Although there was no simple remedy for their rowdiness, the presence of their wives and children had a tempering effect, as did the influx of a civilian population.

Among the civilian population migrating to Pensacola during the second Spanish period were Mariana Bonifay and Charles Lavalle, both of whom left an indelible mark on the town. The French-born Mariana arrived in 1781 with a husband, Joseph Bonifay, and three children. Once a resident in Pensacola she and Joseph added three more children to the brood. The Bonifays became real estate speculators and developers, entering into a partnership with Charles Lavalle in 1790. After Joseph Bonifay's death in 1800, Mariana continued the business partnership with Charles Lavalle and forged a personal relationship as well—one that produced four more children. The offspring of Bonifay and Lavalle married into other prominent Pensacola families, giving birth to the town's social elite.

The Bonifay and Lavalle clan, like many French and Spanish residents, were Catholic. American families migrating to West Florida generally were not, but these Anglo Protestants were welcomed so long as they practiced their faith in private. It is unlikely that Protestants migrating into the colony were ever persecuted for their religion or made to feel isolated because of their faith. Pensacola Catholics were notoriously lax in practicing theirs. As an example, only seven parishioners of Saint Michael's Parish took communion on Easter Sunday in 1790, but they were enthusiastic devotees of the boisterous street celebrations that marked feast days on the Church calendar. During the week leading up to Easter, for example, residents hung Judas Iscariot in effigy and shot him with rifles and pistols at week's end.[5]

An Irish priest, James Coleman, ministered to this apathetic/enthusiastic flock for almost three decades, from 1794 to 1822. The last and longest serving in a series of priests, Coleman shamed local officials into building a church, reciting for them the chapter, book, and verse of the Laws of the Indies: "from time immemorial, a church was meant for this proposed position [on Ferdinand Plaza] based on the ancient figure of the town and as most compliant with the spirit of the law 8, title 7, book 4 of the Digest of the Indies." With the addition of a church, Pensacola became a proper Spanish town.

Settlement

Present at the Battle of Pensacola in 1781, Francisco Saavedra de Sangronis recorded in his journal that Pensacola was a "lovely" town not unlike Kingston, Jamaica, with delightful wooden houses arranged on spacious streets and squares.[6] The picturesque town was basically the one that British surveyor Elias Durnford designed in 1764. It contained some 200 houses fronted by streets of sand. Initially, the Spanish did little other than rename the existing streets. Many of the town lots remained vacant giving the town an airy, open feel. But the influx of settlers in the aftermath of the Louisiana Purchase did fill in some of the vacant lots around town. Two extant structures remain from this period: the simple Creole cottage owned by Julee Panton and the more formal one built by Mariana Bonifay and Charles Lavalle.

Over time, however, the sense of order established by the British surveyor Elias Durnford in 1764, and apparent to the Spanish official Francisco Saavedra in 1781, eroded. Local officials neglected to maintain the old fort at the center of town, allowing the walls to fall down, sold the weed-infested garden plots to the north of town at public auctions, and labored to resolve frequent disputes over lot ownership. Against this backdrop, Vicente Pintado, surveyor general of Spanish west Florida from 1805 to 1817, arrived to correct the "great disorder and confusion in relations to lots and streets, their dimensions and directions." Pintado redefined property lines, corrected irregular street patterns, divided the town into "wards," and designated ap-

PLATE 5.4. The Julee Cottage on its original site. From the collection of West Florida Historic Preservation, Inc.

PLATE 5.5. The Lavalle House relocated to Historic Pensacola Village. From the collection of West Florida Historic Preservation, Inc.

FIGURE 5.2. The Division of the Four Wards. A Plan of Pensacola 1827. Digitized and adapted from map on file at John C. Pace Library, Special Collections, University of West Florida, Pensacola.

proximately thirty acres of fort grounds for development. Pintado reserved the northern portion of the old fort for residences, the central portion for government buildings, and the eastern and western sections for open spaces, which evolved into Seville Square and Plaza Ferdinand today.[7] All residents had to petition for recognition of property ownership. Catholic residents also petitioned for a twenty-five-acre parcel, in proximity to the old British burial ground, which became St. Michael's Cemetery. Although officially recognized in 1810, the cemetery like the rest of the town, was well established prior to any formal designation.

The town property of Panton, Leslie and Company was among those resurveyed by Vincente Pintado. William Panton's house in the western ward, along the bay shore, reflected both his standing in the Pensacola society and the importance of his company to the West Florida economy. The imposing, three-storied brick structure with glass windows, a veranda, three chimneys, and imported furniture took up several lots. His neighbors in this western ward, the ethnic and racially mixed lot mentioned above, like most other residents of Pensacola, had come to depend on the commodities that his company sold in town under the auspices of the Indian trade.[8]

FIGURE 5.3. Panton Leslie-John Forbes Trading House. Photograph ca. 1906. From the collection of West Florida Historic Preservation, Inc.

Survival

Writing in 1781, Francisco Saavedra predicted that Pensacola "will again become as useless and burdensome to the Spaniards as it was before it was ceded to the English if an effort is not made to trade with the Indians." Although the Spanish failed to maintain the broader economic prosperity established under the British, they made concessions to ensure the continuation of the Indian trade. In 1789, officials granted Panton, Leslie and Company a monopoly on the deerskin trade in West Florida and the right to sell some goods to the general population.

Historical documents suggest that the company sold a great many goods under the guise of the Indian trade. Included on a "List of Goods for the Indian Trade of Panton, Leslie and Company" were black pepper, cheese, mustard, spices, beer, cider, medicine, sugar, coffee, tea, butter, salted beef, salt pork, salmon, ham, wine, candles, porcelain, and glassware. Local officials were supposed to "keep a watchful eye on goods introduced by Panton, Leslie and Company." However, officials who were expected to monitor the company were engaged in illicit trade themselves. As always, the frontier environment facilitated trade networks not sanctioned by any government.

Not all commodities were imported or smuggled. At the Pensacola Tivoli, guests dined on local fare of beef, rabbit, chicken, fish, crab, turtle, oyster, and conch. Vegetables may not have been in abundance, but one particularly fragrant fruit was: peaches. Flourishing in the sandy soils in and around

Pensacola, peaches might well have been planted around the Tivoli House, much as oranges were planted around the New Orleans Tivoli, for consumption as well as for fragrance. Peach pits, which survive well in the archaeological record, are recovered on almost all colonial sites in Pensacola, including that of the Tivoli.

Thanks to men like John B. Cazenave, Pedro Bardinave, Rene Chardiveneau, and William Panton, Pensacola residents had access to entertainment, food, drink, and luxury items not often available for purchase in a remote Spanish colonial town. Theirs was not simply an existence that bridged the interim between the British colonial and American territorial periods. Theirs was a rich life, characterized by openness and toleration. Nonetheless, these increasingly cosmopolitan residents of Pensacola were about to be swept up in the tide of American expansion.

Waning of Spanish Authority

That the second Spanish period of Pensacola's history should come to an inglorious end was not foretold in 1781. In the years following the American Revolutionary War, the Spanish empire was on the mend and the United States was hampered by growing pains. However, when Charles III died in 1788 and Charles IV (1788–1808) came to the Spanish throne with little administrative experience or judgment, Spain's prospects dimmed. The new king quickly proved a poor replacement for his most capable father. Within a few years, Charles's inexperienced advisors entangled Spain in a disastrous war with revolutionary France. Spain sued for peace in 1795, the same year in which it ceded a considerable portion of West Florida, that above the 31st parallel, to the United States in what was known as Pickney's Treaty. The treaty is a testament to American strength and Spanish weakness, which was about to become ever more apparent in the Louisiana Purchase of 1803.

Thomas Jefferson had been satisfied with, even comforted by, the fact that Louisiana was Spanish and that Spain had a policy of inviting in Anglo-American settlers. "Till our population can be sufficiently advanced [in numbers] to gain it from them piece by piece," it could not "be in better hands." The Spanish naively believed that Anglo Americans migrating into West Florida would be loyal subjects. Thomas Jefferson famously likened the idea to "settling the Goths at the gates of Rome" and wished "a hundred thousand of our inhabitants would accept the invitation," thus "delivering to us peacefully what may otherwise cost us a war."[9]

Jefferson's comfort level with Spanish Louisiana evaporated in 1802 when he learned that the vast colony had "reverted" to France two years earlier in a secret treaty. Napoleon subsequently sold Louisiana to the Americans in 1803, easing Jefferson's concerns and stirring his curious mind, while striking fear in the hearts of Spanish officials across the Atlantic. A young, aggressive republic was suddenly within striking distance of the silver mines of northern Mexico. Americans soon added insult to Spanish injury by claiming that the Louisiana Purchase encompassed a good portion of West Florida as well, all the way to the Perdido River, the modern-day Alabama-Florida border. The Americans made good on that claim in the War of 1812.

Many American officials saw in the War of 1812 the opportunity to annex the Floridas, and this played out during the war. Mobile fell to the Americans in 1813, when James Wilkinson invaded West Florida and captured the strategic Alabama port city, leaving Pensacola isolated. Andrew Jackson made matters worse in 1814 and 1818 when he invaded the colony, capturing Pensacola on each occasion. In 1814, Jackson did so under the pretext of British intrigue in the port town: the British were there recruiting Indians and blacks, arming them, and training them. Jackson invaded in November of that year and forced the British to abandon the town. On this occasion, the American general did not hold Pensacola, as he lacked the support of officials in Washington, D.C., for such a move and had pressing business in Louisiana. Jackson moved on to fight the most decisive battle of the war at New Orleans in December 1814. Had he not departed for the Crescent City, Pensacola might have remained under American control, just as Mobile did from 1813. The 1814 occupation of Pensacola, however, hastened the end of the Spanish era.

Andrew Jackson returned to West Florida in 1818, this time in pursuit of Indians who had raided Georgia and were rumored to have taken refuge in Pensacola. As Jackson's army approached the outer redoubts of the town in May 1818, his men skirmished with Spanish troops under the command of Governor José Masot. The latter dropped back to Fort San Carlos de Barrancas, virtually abandoning Pensacola to the invaders. After a fierce battle at Fort Barrancas on the night of May 25 and the morning of May 26, the outmanned Masot surrendered. Subsequently, Jackson loaded the Spanish soldiers, officials, their families, and their archives aboard a ship bound for Havana. En route, the ship was captured and plundered of its contents, resulting in the loss of much of the recorded history of Pensacola's Second Spanish Period.

The futures of Jackson and Masot further mirror American fortunes and Spanish misfortunes. Jackson went on to become a territorial governor, a senator, and finally president. Masot died a broken man. In 1819, after being captured by pirates off the coast of Yucatan, Masot was under house arrest in Cuba, pending an investigation into his surrender at Pensacola. In November 1820, one week before the verdict was to be returned, he died, having spent the last months of his life deranged and in solitary confinement.[10] In February 1819 the Spanish returned to Pensacola, but negotiations for the transfer of the town to American control were already under way.

In 1821, the U.S. Senate ratified the Adams-Onís Treaty, the basis for the official transfer of the Spanish Floridas to the Americans. Andrew Jackson arrived in Pensacola—on this his third visit—to accept East and West Florida on behalf of his government. The formal ceremony took place on July 17, 1821, and all Spanish subjects were encouraged to relocate to Cuba. On July 23, 1821, Rachel Jackson sat down to write a letter to her friend Eliza Kingsley. Although Jackson disparaged the departing Spaniards and the solitary town they left behind, she was captivated by the bay: "The most beautiful water prospect I ever saw; and from ten o'clock in the morning until ten at night we have the finest sea breeze. There is something in it so exhilarating, so pure, so wholesome, it enlivens the whole system." In Rachel Jackson's glowing assessment of Pensacola Bay and its environs, one hears echoes of a tribute penned by Carlos de Sigüenza y Góngora in 1693.

Summary

The physical evidence of the first 222 years of Pensacola's recorded history (1559–1781) is limited to the archaeological record, but the Second Spanish Period can be seen in extant structures around town—in St. Michael's Cemetery and in Historic Pensacola Village. A walk through the historic cemetery, an outdoor museum in the middle of a modern urban environment, unveils a past rich in cultural diversity. A stroll through the historic village exposes one to the Julee Cottage and the Lavalle House. Moved to their current location, preserved, and open to the public, these structures are wonderful examples of Creole-style architecture and of the entrepreneurial spirit of settlers in the twilight of the Spanish era.

The original Tivoli House endured into the American territorial period. Used by the Spanish to store artillery and ammunition in anticipation of American aggression in 1817–1818, the Tivoli suffered considerable damage. Restored in the aftermath of the conflict, it embraced another arena of entertainment: the theater. Throughout its existence, the Tivoli House served as the center of entertainment in Pensacola, providing food, drinks, and amusement to a diverse clientele.

PLATE 5.6. Gateway into historic St. Michael's Cemetery. Courtesy of St. Michael's Cemetery Foundation of Pensacola, Inc.

RECIPE: Gaspache Salad

During the Second Spanish occupation of Pensacola, the population became quite diverse and cosmopolitan. Small kitchen gardens and peaceful trade supplied a variety of vegetables to the population of the town. All the ingredients for cool, refreshing *gazpacho* (cold vegetable soup) were readily available and led to the development of a recipe unique to Pensacola. In place of baked bread, the Pensacola Spanish used hardtack biscuits. While methods of preparation, some ingredients, and garnishes may vary slightly among local families, a version of this popular bread salad is still served in many Pensacola homes today—offering a tasty blend of Old and New World flavors and tradition!

6 hardtack biscuits (see chapter 1 for hardtack recipe)
1 quart Hellmann's (or homemade) mayonnaise
2–3 cloves garlic, minced
4–6 medium ripe tomatoes
2 large green bell peppers
2–4 cucumbers
3 white onions
3 ribs celery, "strings" removed
½ cup wine vinegar
Water
Salt
Paprika
1 green bell pepper, sliced, for garnish

Soak hardtack in water (just to cover) and vinegar until very soft—about two hours. Squeeze as much liquid as possible out of the hardtack and put the bread in a colander to finish draining. Meanwhile, slice the tomatoes, bell peppers, cucumbers, and onions very thinly. Chop or slice celery. Peel and mince garlic (or use a garlic press).

To assemble the salad, use a large, deep casserole or similar container and spread a layer of crumbled hardtack over the bottom; sprinkle that with half of the celery and half of the minced garlic. Cover with plenty of mayonnaise; salt generously. Add a layer of tomato, then a layer of cucumber, salt, and another layer of mayonnaise. Then layer sliced onion and bell pepper; cover with mayonnaise and salt. Repeat the entire process, ending with a layer of crumbled hardtack covered by mayonnaise. Garnish with paprika and bell pepper rings. Refrigerate eight to ten hours; serve very cold. Makes fourteen to sixteen servings—background and recipe by Catherine Parker.

Conclusion

Carlos de Sigüenza's tribute to Pensacola Bay in 1693—"the finest jewel possessed by His Majesty . . . not only here in America but in all his kingdom"—may seem to the modern reader nothing more than the musings of an old man or the exaggerations of a baroque intellectual known for hyperbole. However, Sigüenza's assessment of the bay was in line with the perceptions of his contemporaries and those who came before and after him: for almost 300 years, kings, intellectuals, bureaucrats, priests, sailors, and the wife of an American president concluded that Pensacola Bay was most extraordinary. The bay's attributes as a deepwater, sheltered harbor often put it at the center of a struggle for empire in the colonial Atlantic World.

Before Spaniards, Frenchmen, the British, and Americans coveted Pensacola Bay, Native Americans did. They came to the pristine bay to harvest the abundant marine life that lived in its warm waters and the animals that abounded in the piney woods ringing its shores. Whereas Indians moved in and out of the bay's environs and settled along sheltered, interior streams and rivers, Europeans set up permanent settlements on the bay itself: sometimes on a bluff, sometimes on a barrier island, but always in an exposed location, and too often in the path of tropical hurricanes.

Tristán de Luna, founder of the first Pensacola settlement, got a lesson in the history-altering power of a hurricane in September 1559. Had the hurricane not destroyed Luna's fledgling colony (1559–1561), the history of the American Southeast might have been different. Spain's failure to establish a permanent settlement on the Gulf Coast in an era when it enjoyed a monopoly in the New World forever compromised its enterprise of colonization in the region.

By the time the Spanish returned to Pensacola Bay in 1698, they had to compete with both the French and the English. In that year, Andrés de Arriola, the founder of First Pensacola, Santa María de Galve (1698–1719), carved out a tenuous foothold in the hotly contested Gulf region. By then, however, the French and English claimed colonies stretching from Canada to the Caribbean and hungrily eyed Louisiana and Georgia, which they colonized in 1699 and 1733, respectively.

Arriola's successors faced ever greater challenges from Spain's European rivals. Long before Georgia was founded, the Carolina English and their Creek allies waged war on the Spanish in West Florida. In the War of Spanish Succession, the British and Creeks vanquished Apalachee province but could not capture Pensacola. Presidio residents held out against the English onslaught only to fall to the French in the War of the Quadruple Alliance. After a brief French interlude (1719–1722), the Spanish returned to the bay, taking up residence in Presidio Santa Rosa Pensacola (1722–1752). Living on a barrier island, they were less susceptible (although not immune) to Indian attacks but more vulnerable to hurricanes and their accompanying tidal surges. Following a particularly devastating hurricane in November 1752, island residents relocated to the mainland where they founded the short-lived Presidio San Miguel (1757–1763). In 1763, the Spanish abandoned the town to the English.

After 1763, Pensacola evolved from a Spanish frontier outpost into a proper British town (1763–1781). The surveyor general of the colony of West Florida, Elias Durnford, laid out a grid that is the basis for the modern city of Pensacola. British officials believed that they could succeed where the Spanish had failed and make West Florida a profitable commercial enterprise. And to a certain extent, they did, creating a vibrant economy in the naval stores industry and the deerskin trade.

When the Spanish returned to Pensacola in 1781, they attempted to maintain the economic prosperity that the British had developed, particularly with regard to naval stores. In this endeavor they failed. The Spanish also failed to hold back the tide of American influence that swept over West Florida and Pensacola in the years following Bernardo de Gálvez's triumph over the British. However, in the midst of growing American influence Panton, Leslie and Company emerged as the dominant Indian trading company in the Southeast and the major commercial interest in Spanish West Florida, trading British goods for deerskin. And through immigration Pensacola evolved into one of the most diverse societies in North America.

Those who gathered at the Tivoli House in the twilight of the Spanish era could gaze upon the sparkling waters of the bay, the same waters that stirred individuals as diverse as Carlos de Sigüenza and Rachel Jackson to giddy enthusiasm. Jackson's 1821 assessment of Pensacola Bay—"The most beautiful water prospect I ever saw"—confirms that this jewel of the northern Gulf Coast had lost none of the luster that caught Sigüenza's eye in 1693. One need only cast an eye on the bay's shimmering waters while crossing the Pensacola Bay Bridge to recognize that it has lost none of its allure in 450 years. This beauty of a natural harbor still stirs the senses and enlivens the spirit and continues to captivate the imagination of archaeologists and historians who are working to preserve its rich cultural heritage.

NOTES

Introduction

1. Bense, *Archaeology of the Southeastern United States*, 9–24.

CHAPTER ONE. *First Settlement, 1559–1561*

1. Hoffman, *Florida's Frontiers*, 38–39.
2. The classic narrative of the Luna settlement, which informs this chapter, is Priestly, *Tristán De Luna.*
3. Weddle, *Spanish Sea*, 257–60.
4. Priestly, *Tristán De Luna*, 81–84.
5. Hudson et al., "The Tristan De Luna Expedition," 124–25.
6. Discussion of Emanuel Point archaeological assemblage, except where noted, is summarized from Smith et al., "The Emanuel Point Ship: Archaeological Investigations, 1992–1995," and "The Emanuel Point Ship Archaeological Investigations, 1997–1998."
7. Reitz and Scarry, *Reconstructing Historic Subsistence*, 26–38.
8. Arnade, "Tristan De Luna and Ochuse," 213–14.
9. See *Codice Osuna.*
10. Lowery, *The Spanish Settlements*, 362–67.
11. Priestly, *Tristán De Luna*, 164.
12. Lowery, *The Spanish Settlements*, 369–74.

CHAPTER TWO. *First Pensacola, 1698–1719*

1. Weddle, *The French Thorn*; and Dunn, *Spanish and French Rivalry.*
2. Coker, "Admiral Andres de Pez," 1–10; Leonard, *Spanish Approach to Pensacola*, 19–38.
3. Leonard, *Don Carlos de Sigüenza*; *Spanish Approach*, 38–43.

4. Leonard, "Don Andrés de Arriola," 81–106.
5. Coxe, *A Description of the English Province of Carolana.*
6. For detailed analysis of construction, population, and economy at Santa María de Galve, see Clune, Childers, et al., "Settlement, Settlers, and Survival," 25–82; Coker and Childers, "The Presidio Santa María de Galve," 11–98.
7. From Faye, "The Contest for Pensacola Bay, Part I," 172.
8. Details on the archaeological assemblage of Santa María de Galve, from Bense and Wilson, "Archaeological Remains," 83–209.
9. Harris, "Native Americans of Santa María de Galve"; Harris, "Native Americans," 257–314; Dysart, "Indians in Colonial Pensacola," 61–89.
10. Sims, "Searching for Women at the Presidio Santa María de Galve."
11. On the economy of Presidio Santa María de Galve, see Childers and Cotter, "Arrested Development," 76–103.
12. On trade networks, see Johnson, "Pensacola and Franco/Spanish Trade."
13. From Delanglez, "Documents—M. Le Maire on Louisiana," 150.
14. Hunter, "Historical Archaeology of the Santa Rosa Island Wreck"; and Clune, Childers, et al., "The Wreck of the *Nuestra Señora del Rosario y Santiago Apostol.*"
15. Ford, *The Triangular Struggle*, 107–19.

CHAPTER THREE. *Storms and High Tides, 1722–1763*

1. Archaeological assemblage of presidio Santa Rosa analyzed in Harris et al., "Presidio Isla de Santa Rosa: Archaeological Investigations."
2. Kamen, *Philip V of Spain.*
3. Following discussion of Spanish efforts to reestablish a presence on Pensacola Bay synthesized from Ford, *The Triangular Struggle*, 125–45.
4. Russett, *Dominic Serres*, 10–20.
5. Impacts of the storm on the population of the island presidio analyzed by Clune, Childers, and Whitaker in Harris et al., "Presidio Isla de Santa Rosa."
6. Ford, *Triangular Struggle*, 140–42; Griffith, "The Royal Spanish Presidio of San Miguel," 10–11.
7. Discussion of the mainland settlement of San Miguel, which follows, is taken

from detailed analysis by Clune, Childers, and Bercot in Benchley et al., "The Colonial People of Pensacola," 28–38.

8. Griffith, "The Royal Spanish Presidio of San Miguel de Panzacola," 27–40.
9. Joy, "Excavations under Old Christ Church in Pensacola"; Stringfield and Benchley, "Archaeological Testing of the Old Christ Church Restoration Project"; and Williams, "Land Use at the Site of Old Christ Church."
10. Actions of Miguel Román and Miguel Ortíz Parilla summarized from Benchley et al., "The Colonial People of Pensacola," 20.
11. Coyolillo is the focus of a multifaceted study, Jones and Rowell, eds., *Faces and Voices of Coyolillo.*

CHAPTER FOUR. *British Pensacola, 1763–1781*

1. On the archaeology and history of British Pensacola, see Benchley et al., "The Colonial People of Pensacola."
2. Fabel, *Bombast and Broadside.*
3. Howard, "Early Settlers in British West Florida," 45–55; Siebert, "How the Spaniards Evacuated Pensacola in 1763," 48–57.
4. See Rea and Howard, eds., *The Minutes, Journals, and Acts of the General Assembly of British West Florida.*
5. Stringfield, "Wells in Colonial Pensacola," 21–35.
6. Orrmont, *Diplomat in Warpaint.*
7. Starr, "Campbell Town," 532–47; Howard, *The British Development of West Florida*, 87; and Fabel, *The Economy of British West Florida*, 12–14.
8. Stringfield, "Wells in Colonial Pensacola."
9. Rea, "Graveyard for Britons," 345–64.
10. Discussion of the economy of British West Florida, including that of the Spanish and fur trades which follows, taken from Fabel, *The Economy of British West Florida.*
11. Phillips, "Flood Thy Neighbor," 143–57.
12. For detailed accounts of the Battle of Pensacola, see two book-length treatments: Reparaz, *I Alone*; and Rush, *Spain's Final Triumph.*

CHAPTER FIVE. *Second Spanish Period, 1781–1821*

1. Coker and Inglis, *The Spanish Census of Pensacola*; McAlister, "Pensacola during the Second Spanish Period," 290–91; and Zahendra, "Spanish West Florida," 27–28, 102.
2. This and other quotes of Rachel Jackson taken from, Jackson, "A Letter from Rachel Jackson," 39–42, in McGovern, ed., *Andrew Jackson and Pensacola.*
3. Stringfield, "Wells in Colonial Pensacola," 136–39.
4. Discussion of bureaucrats, settlers, and priests that follows comes from Holmes, "Pensacola Settlers."
5. Crider, "The Borderland Floridas," 19.
6. From Saavedra de Sangronis, *Journal of Don Francisco de Saavedra.*
7. Pintado, *The Papers of Vicente Sebastian Pintado.*
8. Discussion of the Panton, Leslie and Company in this chapter taken from Coker and Watson, *Indian Traders of the Southeastern Spanish Borderlands.*
9. From Owsley and Smith, *Filibusters and Expansionists*, 17.
10. Holmes, "Pensacola Settlers," 27–29.

BIBLIOGRAPHY

Adorno, Rolena and Patrick Charles Pautz, eds. *The Narrative of Cabeza de Vaca.* Lincoln: University of Nebraska Press, 2003.

Arnade, Charles W. "Tristan De Luna and Ochuse (Pensacola Bay) 1559." *Florida Historical Quarterly* 37, no. 3 (January–April 1959): 201–222.

Benchley, Elizabeth, R. Wayne Childers, John James Clune, Cindy L. Bercot, David B. Dodson, April Whitaker, and E. Ashley Flynt. "The Colonial People of Pensacola: History and Archaeology of the Community Associated with Spanish San Miguel de Panzacola (1754–1763) and British Pensacola (1763–1781)," 2 vols. with appendixes. University of West Florida Archaeology Institute, Report of Investigation Number 107. May 2007. Sponsored by the Florida Department of State, Division of Historical Resources.

Bense, Judith A. *Archaeology of the Southeastern United States.* New York: Academic Press, 1994.

———, ed. *Archaeology of Colonial Pensacola.* Gainesville: University Press of Florida, 1999.

———, ed. *Presidio Santa María de Galve: A Struggle for Survival in Early Eighteenth Century Spanish Pensacola.* Gainesville: University Press of Florida, 2004.

Bense, Judith A. and H. James Wilson. "Archaeological Remains." In *Presidio Santa María de Galve: A Struggle for Survival in Early Eighteenth Century Spanish Pensacola*, edited by Judith A. Bense, 83–209. Gainesville: University Press of Florida, 2004.

Born, John Dewey. "British Trade in West Florida, 1763–1783." Ph.D. Dissertation, University of New Mexico, 1963.

Bowden, Jesse Earle, Gordon N. Simons, and Sandra Johnson. *Pensacola: Florida's First Place City. A Pictorial History.* Norfolk: Donning, 1989.

Childers, R. Wayne and Joseph Cotter. "Arrested Development: The Economy of the Royal Presidio of Santa María de Galve." *Gulf South Historical Review* 14 (1998), no. 1: 76–103.

Clayton, Lawrence A., Vernon James Knight, Jr., and Edward C. Moore, eds. *The DeSoto Chronicles: The Expedition of Hernando de Soto to North America in 1539–1543*, 2 vols. Tuscaloosa: University of Alabama Press, 1993.

Clune, John J. "Historical Context and Overview." In *Presidio Santa María De Galve: A Struggle for Survival in Early Eighteenth Century Spanish Pensacola*, edited by Judith A. Bense, 12–24. Gainesville: University Press of Florida, 2004. Clune, John James, R. Wayne Childers, William S. Coker, and Brenda N. Swann. "Settlement, Settlers, and Survival: Documentary Evidence." In *Presidio Santa María De Galve: A Struggle for Survival in Early Eighteenth Century Spanish Pensacola*, edited by Judith A. Bense, 15–82. Gainesville: University Press of Florida, 2004.

Clune, John James, R. Wayne Childers, Hector L. Montford, and Cindy L. Bercot. "The Wreck of the Nuestra Señora del Rosario y Santiago Apostol: Documentary History and Historical Context." March 2003. On file at the University of West Florida Archaeology Institute.

Codice Osuna: Reproducción fascimilar de la obra del mismo titulo, editada en Madrid, 1878, acompañada de 158 páginas inéditas encontradas en el Archivo General de la Nación (México) por Luis Chávez Orozco. Edited by Mariano Téllez-Gíron y Beaufort and Luis Chávez Orozco. Mexico City, 1947.

Coker, William S. "Admiral Andrés de Pez, Pensacola's Hero." In *Santa María de Galve: A Story of Survival*, edited by Virginia Parks, 1–9. Pensacola: Pensacola Historical Society, 1998.

Coker, William S. and R. Wayne Childers. "The Presidio Santa María de Galve: The First Permanent European Settlement on the Northern Gulf Coast." In *Santa María de Galve: A Story of Survival*, edited by Virginia Parks, 11–98. Pensacola: Pensacola Historical Society, 1998.

Coker, William S. and G. Douglas Inglis. *The Spanish Census of Pensacola, 1784–1820: A Genealogical Guide to Spanish Pensacola*. Pensacola: Perdido Bay Press, 1980.

Coker, William S., and Thomas D. Watson. *Indian Traders of the Southeastern Spanish Borderlands: Panton, Leslie and Company and John Forbes & Company, 1783–1847*. Gainesville: University Presses of Florida; University of West Florida Press, 1986.

Coleman, James C. and Irene S. Coleman. *Guardians of the Gulf: Pensacola Fortifications, 1698–1980*. Pensacola: Pensacola Historical Society, 1982.

Cox, Beverly and Martin Jacobs. "Body, Mind & Spirit: Native Cooking of the Americas." *Native Peoples Magazine*, 2004.

Coxe, Daniel. *A Description of the English Province of Carolana, by the Spaniards called Florida, and by the French La Louisiane*. Introduction by William S. Coker. Gainesville: University of Florida Press, 1976.

Crider, Robert Franklin. "The Borderland Floridas, 1815–1821: Spanish Sovereignty under Siege." M.A. Thesis, Florida State University, 1979.

Delanglez, Jean. "Documents—M. Le Maire on Louisiana." *Mid America: A Historical Review* 19, no. 4 (1937): 124–52.

Dunn, William E. *Spanish and French Rivalry in the Gulf Region of the United States, 1678–1702: The Beginnings of Texas and Pensacola*. Austin: University of Texas, 1917.

Dysart, Jane. "Indians in Colonial Pensacola." In *Archaeology of Colonial Pensacola*, edited by Judith E. Bense, 61–89. Gainesville: University Press of Florida, 1999.

Fabel, Robin F. A. *Bombast and Broadside: The Lives of George Johnstone*. Tuscaloosa: University of Alabama Press, 1987.

———. *The Economy of British West Florida, 1763–1783*. Tuscaloosa: University of Alabama Press, 1988.

Faye, Stanley. "The Contest for Pensacola Bay and Other Gulf Ports, 1698–1722, Part I." *Florida Historical Quarterly* 24, no. 3 (January 1946): 167–195.

———. "The Contest for Pensacola Bay and Other Gulf Ports, 1698–1722, Part II." *Florida Historical Quarterly* 24, no. 4 (January 1946): 302–328.

Flynt, Elizabeth Ashley. "A Study of Households Occupied in British and Second Spanish Pensacola, 1763–1821." M.A. Thesis, University of West Florida, 2004.

Ford, Lawrence Carroll. *The Triangular Struggle for Spanish Pensacola, 1689–1739*. Washington, D.C.: Catholic University of America Press, 1939.

Gannon, Michael. *The New History of Florida*. Gainesville: University Press of Florida, 1996.

Gold, Robert L. *Borderland Empires in Transition; the Triple-Nation Transfer of Florida*. Carbondale: Southern Illinois University Press, 1969.

Griffen, William B. "Spanish Pensacola, 1700–1763." *Florida Historical Quarterly* 37, no. 3 (January–April 1959): 242–262.

Griffith, Wendell Lamar. "The Royal Spanish Presidio of San Miguel De Panzacola, 1753–1763." M.A. Thesis, University of West Florida, 1988.

Harris, Norma J. "Native Americans of Santa María de Galve." M.A. Thesis, University of West Florida, 1999.

———. "Native Americans." In *Presidio Santa María De Galve: A Struggle for Survival in Early Eighteenth Century Spanish Pensacola*, edited by Judith A. Bense, 257–314. Gainesville: University Press of Florida, 2004.

Harris, Norma J., Krista L. Eschbach, Judith A. Bense, John J. Clune, R. Wayne Childers, Janet R. Lloyd, Catherine Parker, Marissa C. Condosta, Jorge A. Provenzali, Mary M. Furlong, April A. Holmes, Kristy M. Mickwee, James N. Greene, Julie R. Comerford, Jennifer Melcher, and April L. Whitaker. "Presidio Isla de Santa Rosa: Archaeological Investigations 2002–2004." Report prepared for Gulf Islands National Seashore, National Park Service. University of West Florida Archaeology Institute, Report of Investigation Number 133. July 2006. Sponsored by the Florida Department of State, Division of Historical Resources.

Hoffman, Paul E. *Florida's Frontiers*. Bloomington: Indiana University Press, 2002.

Holmes, Jack. "Pensacola Settlers, 1781–1821." Pensacola: Historic Pensacola Preservation Board, n.d.; unpublished manuscript digitized from original source held at University of West Florida Special Collections and available online in the Florida Heritage Collection.

Howard, Clinton Newton. *The British Development of West Florida, 1763–1769*. Berkeley: University of California Press, 1947.

———. "Early Settlers in British West Florida." *Florida Historical Quarterly* 24, no. 1 (July 1945): 45–55.

Hudson, Charles, Marvin T. Smith, Chester B. DePratter, and Emilia Kelley. "The Tristan De Luna Expedition, 1559–1561." In *First Encounters: Spanish Explorations in the Caribbean and the United States, 1492–1570*, edited by Jerald T. Milanich and Susan Milbrath. Gainesville: University Press of Florida and Florida Museum of Natural History, 1989.

Hunter, James W. "Historical Archaeology of the Santa Rosa Island Wreck." M.A. Thesis, University of West Florida, 2001.

Johnson, Cecil. *British West Florida*. New Haven: Yale University Press, 1943.

Johnson, Sandra L. "Pensacola and Franco-Spanish Trade and Interaction on the Northern Gulf." M.A. Thesis, University of West Florida, 1999.

Jones, Marcus D. and Charles Henry Rowell, eds. *Faces and Voices of Coyolillo, an Afromestizo Pueblo in Mexico*. Special issue of *Callaloo* 27, no. 1 (Winter 2004).

Joy, Deborah. "Excavations under Old Christ Church in Pensacola, Florida." Report on file at University of West Florida Archaeology Institute, 1989.

Kamen, Henry. *Philip V of Spain: The King Who Reigned Twice.* New Haven: Yale University Press, 2001.

Leonard, Irving A. "Don Andres de Arriola and the Occupation of Pensacola." In *New Spain and the Anglo American West: Historical Contributions Presented to Herbert Eugene Bolton*, edited by George P. Hammond, 81–106. Lancaster, PA: Lancaster Press, 1932.

———. *Don Carlos de Sigüenza: A Mexican Savant of the Seventeenth Century.* Berkeley: University of California Press, 1929.

———. *Spanish Approach to Pensacola, 1689–1693.* Albuquerque: Quivira Society, 1939.

Lloyd, Robert B., Jr. "Development of the Plan of Pensacola during the Colonial Era, 1559–1821." *Florida Historical Quarterly* 64, no. 3 (January 1986): 254–273.

López-Oña, Fifi Obregón, ed. *De Nuestra Mesa: Our Food, Wine and Tradition.* Palm Beach, FL: New Hope Charities, 1998.

Lowery, Woodbury. *The Spanish Settlements within the Present Limits of the United States, 1513–1561.* New York: Knickerbocker Press, 1901.

Lyon, Eugene. "Spain's Sixteenth-Century North American Settlement Attempts: A Neglected Aspect." *Florida Historical Quarterly* 59, no. 3 (January 1981): 275–291.

McAlister, L. N. "Pensacola during the Second Spanish Period." *Florida Historical Quarterly* 37, no. 3 (January 1959): 281–336.

McGovern, James R., ed. *Andrew Jackson and Pensacola.* Pensacola: Tom White the Printer, 1974.

Orrmont, Arthur. *Diplomat in Warpaint: Chief Alexander McGillivray of the Creeks.* London: Abelard-Schuman, 1968.

Owsley, Frank Lawrence and Gene A. Smith. *Filibusters and Expansionists: Jeffersonian Manifest Destiny, 1800–1821.* Tuscaloosa: University of Alabama Press, 1997.

Parker, Catherine Branson. "Foodways and Faunal Remains at Presidio Santa María de Galve, 1698–1719: Between the Devil and the Deep Blue Sea." M.A. Thesis, University of West Florida, 2001.

Parks, Virginia. *Pensacola: Spaniards to the Space Age.* Pensacola: Pensacola Historical Society, 1986.

———, ed. *Santa María De Galve: A Story of Survival.* Pensacola: Pensacola Historical Society, 1998.

Phillips, John. "Flood Thy Neighbor: Colonial and American Water-Powered Mills in West Florida." Unpublished paper presented at the Sixteenth Gulf South History and Humanities Conference, Pensacola, Florida, October 1997.

Pintado, Vicente Sebastian. *The Papers of Vicente Sebastián Pintado.* Microform Collection on file in Special Collections Department, University of West Florida Libraries, published 1841–1842.

Priestley, Herbert Ingram. *The Luna Papers: Documents Relating to the Expedition of Don Tristán De Luna Y Arellano for the Conquest of La Florida in 1559–1561.* 2 vols. De Land: Florida State Historical Society, 1928.

———. *Tristán De Luna, Conquistador of the Old South: A Study in Spanish Imperial Policy.* Glendale, CA: Arthur H. Clark, 1936.

Rea, Robert R. "'Graveyard for Britons,' West Florida, 1763–1781." *Florida Historical Quarterly* 47, no. 4 (April 1969): 345–364.

Rea, Robert R. and Milo B. Howard. *The Minutes, Journals, and Acts of the General Assembly of British West Florida.* Tuscaloosa: University of Alabama Press, 1979.

Reitz, Elizabeth J. and C. Margaret Scarry. *Reconstructing Historic Subsistence with an Example from Sixteenth-Century Spanish Florida.* Society for Historical Archaeology, Special Publication Series, no. 3, 1985.

Renacker, George Michael. "A Study of Military Architecture for Fort San Carlos de Austria at Santa María de Galve." M.A. Thesis, University of West Florida, 2001.

Reparaz, Carmen de. *I Alone: Bernardo de Gálvez and the Taking of Pensacola in 1781: A Spanish Contribution to the Independence of the United States.* Madrid: Ediciones de Cultura Hispánica, 1993.

Romans, Bernard. *A Concise and Natural History of East and West Florida.* Introduction by Kathryn E. Holland Braund. Tuscaloosa: University of Alabama Press, 1999.

Rush, Nixon Orwin. *Spain's Final Triumph over Great Britain in the Gulf of Mexico: The Battle of Pensacola, March 9 to May 8, 1781.* Florida State University Studies, no. 48. Tallahassee: Florida State University, 1966.

Russett, Alan. *Dominic Serres R. A: 1719–1793 War Artist to the Navy.* London: Antique Collector's Club, 2001.

Saavedra de Sangronis, Francisco. *Journal of Don Francisco de Saavedra de Sangronis*

1780–1783. Edited and introduced by Francisco Morales Padrón; translated by Aileen Moore Topping. Gainesville: University Press of Florida, 1989.

Siebert, Wilbur H. "How the Spaniards Evacuated Pensacola in 1763." *Florida Historical Quarterly* 11, no. 2 (October 1932), *48*–57.

Serres, Dominic. *An Account of the First Discovery and Natural History of Florida*. London: Printed for T. Jerreys, at Charing Cross. 1743 reprinted 1763. Map on file, AGS Collection, University of Wisconsin Milwaukee Library.

Sims, Cynthia Lee Smith. "Searching for Women at the Presidio Santa María de Galve: A New Approach to Examining Women through Material Culture and History." M.A. Thesis, University of West Florida, 2001.

Smith, Roger C., John R. Bratten, J. Cozzi, and Keith Plaskett. "The Emanuel Point Ship Archaeological Investigations, 1997–1998." Tallahassee: Bureau of Archaeological Research, Division of Historical Resources and the University of West Florida, 1998.

Smith, Roger C., James Spirek, John R. Bratten, and Della Scott-Ireton. "The Emanuel Point Ship: Archaeological Investigations, 1992–1995, Preliminary Report." Tallahassee: Bureau of Archaeological Research, Division of Historical Resources Florida, 1995.

South, Stanley, et al. "Spanish Artifacts from Santa Elena." *Anthropological Studies* 7. Columbia: University of South Carolina, Institute of Archaeology and Anthropology, 1988.

Starr, J. Barton. "Campbell Town: French Huguenots in British West Florida." *Florida Historical Quarterly* 54, no.4 (April 1976): 532–47.

Stringfield, Margo S. "Wells in Colonial Pensacola." M.A. Thesis, University of West Florida, 1996.

Stringfield, Margo S. and Elizabeth D. Benchley. "Archaeological Testing of the Old Christ Church Restoration Project." Report on file at University of West Florida Archaeology Institute, 1997.

Swann, Brenda Nancy. "Supplies at Presidio Santa María de Galve (1698–1713): A Study of the Historical and Archaeological Records." M.A. Thesis, University of West Florida, 2000.

Trutter, Marion, ed. *Culinaria Spain*. Cologne, Germany: Konemann Verlagsgesellschaft, 1998.

Weddle, Robert S. *Changing Tides: Twilight and Dawn in the Spanish Sea, 1763–1803*. College Station: Texas A&M University Press, 1995.

———. *The French Thorn: Rival Explorers in the Spanish Sea, 1682–1762*. College Station: Texas A&M Press, 1991.

———. *Spanish Sea: The Gulf of Mexico in North American Discovery, 1500–1685*. College Station: Texas A&M University Press, 1985.

Whitaker, April Leigh. "History and Archaeology at Plaza Ferdinand: An Analysis of Spanish and British Colonial Lifeways." M.A. Thesis, University of West Florida, 2005.

Williams, Carrie A. "Land Use at the Site of Old Christ Church, Pensacola, Florida." M.A. Thesis, University of West Florida, 2004.

Wood, Peter H., Gregory A. Waselkov, and M. Thomas Hatley. *Powhatan's Mantle: Indians in the Colonial Southeast*. Lincoln and London: University of Nebraska Press, 1989.

Zahendra, Peter. "Spanish West Florida, 1781–1821." Ph.D. Dissertation, University of Michigan, 1976.

INDEX

Margo S. Stringfield is an archaeologist at the University of West Florida Archaeology Institute.

John J. Clune Jr. is a historian and administrator at the University of West Florida.